RED SOX

BOSTON

Carl

YASTRZEMSKI

★ GOLDEN GLOVER

★ M.V.P.

★ "CAPTAIN CARL"

★ '67 TRIPLE CROWN WINNER

BOSTON RED SOX

CARL YASTRZEMSKI '61-'83

★ 400 HOME RUNS

★ 3000 HITS

★ 18 ALL STAR GAMES

★ '67-'75 WORLD SERIES

YAZ

#8

FENWAY PARK

RUGGED LAND | 401 WEST STREET · SECOND FLOOR · NEW YORK CITY · NY 10014 · USA

YASTRZEMSKI

BY

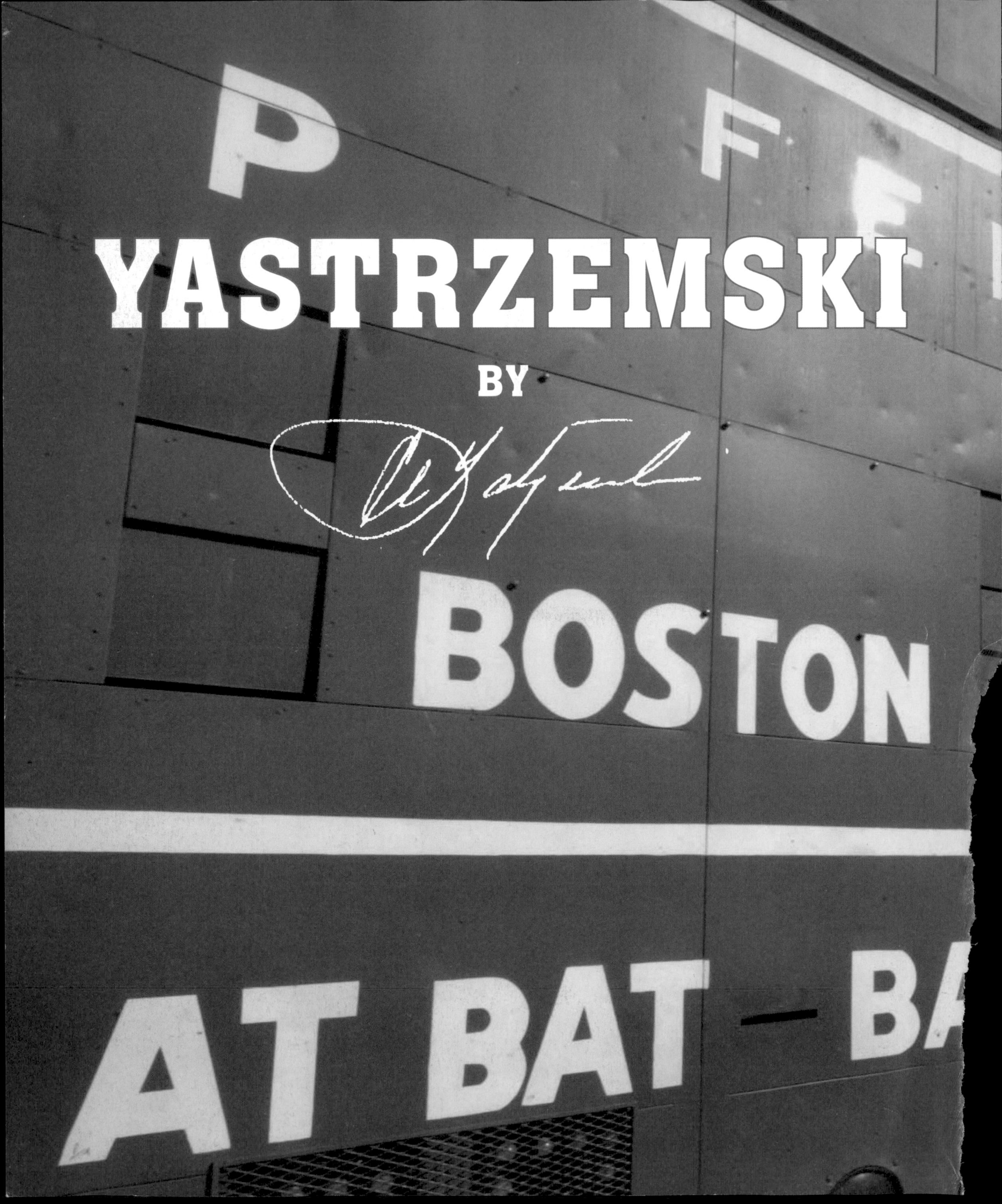

RuggedLand

PUBLISHED BY RUGGED LAND, LLC

401 WEST STREET · SECOND FLOOR · NEW YORK CITY · NY 10014 · USA

RUGGED LAND and colophon are trademarks of Rugged Land, LLC.

Library of Congress Cataloging-in-Publication Data

Yastrzemski, Carl.
Yastrzemski / by Carl Yastrzemski. -- 1st ed.
p. cm.
ISBN-13: 978-1-59071-089-0
ISBN-10: 1-59071-089-4
1. Yastrzemski, Carl. 2. Baseball players--United States--Biography.
3. Boston Red Sox (Baseball team)--History. I. Title.
GV865.Y35Y37 2007
796.357092--dc22
[B]
2007006470

Book Design by
HSU + ASSOCIATES

RUGGED LAND WEBSITE ADDRESS: WWW.RUGGEDLAND.COM

TABLE OF CONTENTS

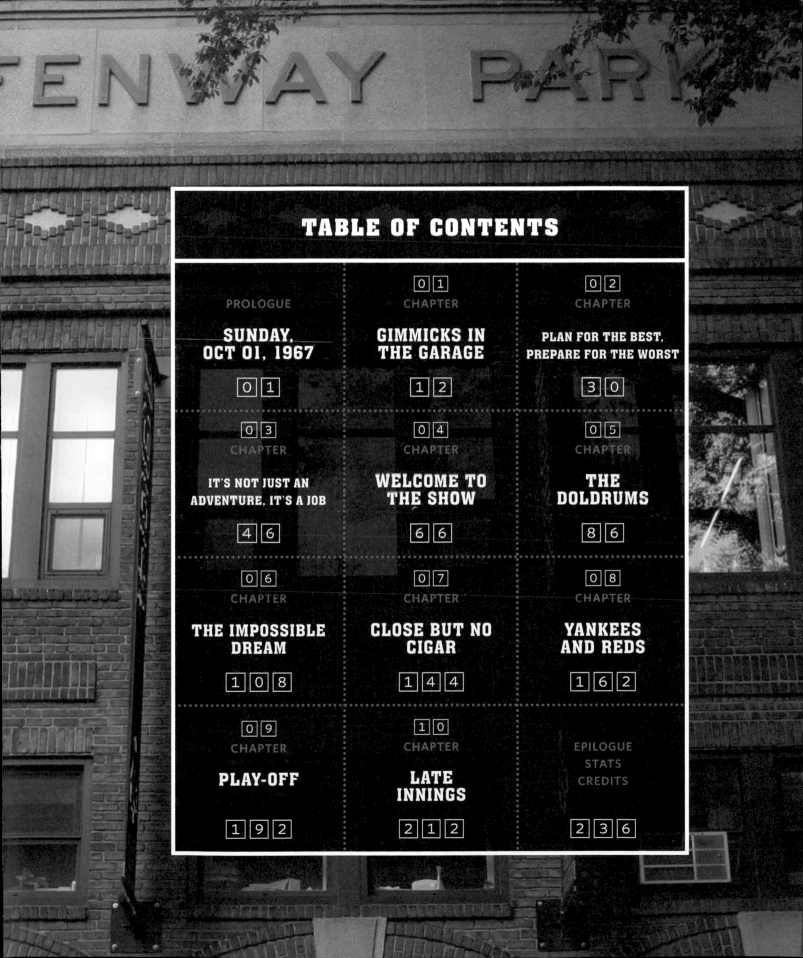

OTHER TITLES BY CARL YASTRZEMSKI

Yaz

BY CARL YASTRZEMSKI AND AL HIRSHBERG

Batting

BY CARL YASTRZEMSKI AND AL HIRSHBERG

Yaz: Baseball, the Wall and Me

BY CARL YASTRZEMSKI AND GERALD ESKENAZI

DEDICATION

*For my mother and father
who were my inspiration
throughout my baseball career.*

LIFE

Brazen Empire of Crime, PART II HOW THE MOB MUSCLES INTO YOUR DAILY LIFE

The Frenzied Pennant Race

Carl Yastrzemski, Boston's slugger, singles against Chicago

SEPTEMBER 8 · 1967 · 35¢

SUNDAY, OCTOBER 1, 1967

I couldn't sleep.

Lying in the dark, it was like a weight was pressing down on my chest. I had to get out of there.

I slipped out of bed and dressed lightly.

I stepped out into the October dawn. Alone in the thin light, I walked around the golf course for twenty minutes, just trying to clear my head. I was finally starting to breathe OK. I realized I was freezing, though. Getting in my car, I turned on the heat and started driving. I got on Route 128. Soon I found myself steering through the empty, shuttered streets of Gloucester. I rolled to a stop sign and stayed there. My grip closed up on the top of the wheel. Twisting my hands, I leaned in, eyes in a thousand-yard stare.

Dean Chance is going to kill me...who did I think I was kidding? The Twins are a better ball club...it's all up to me and I can't do it!

A car honked behind me.

How long had I been sitting here?

I took a deep breath, exhaled and pulled away, heading back towards Boston.

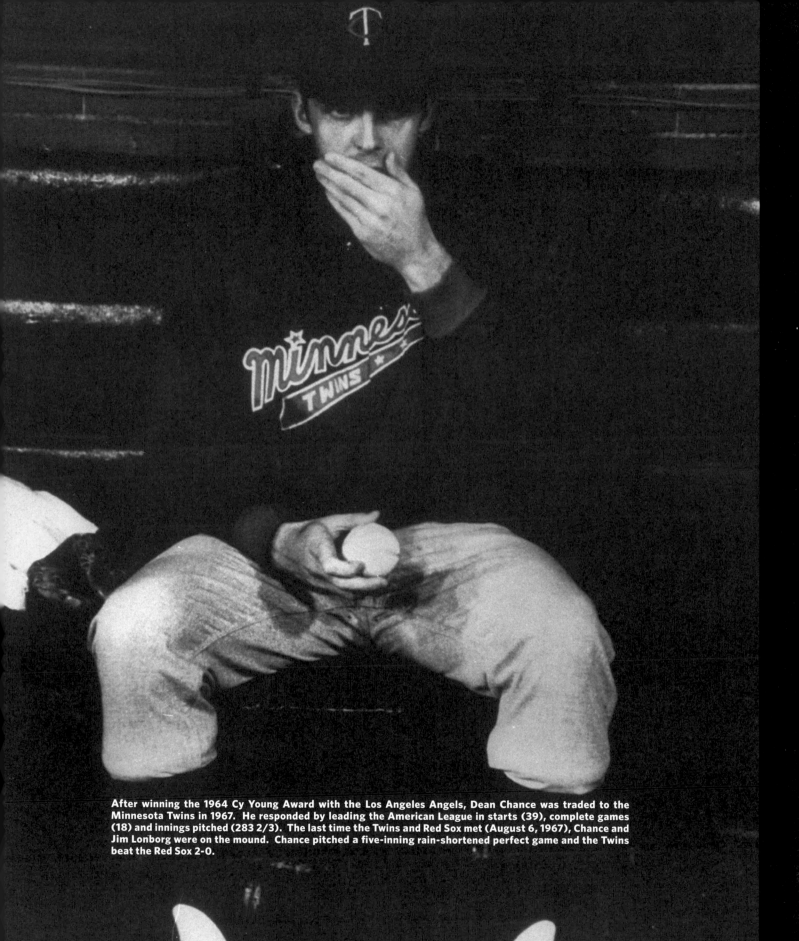

After winning the 1964 Cy Young Award with the Los Angeles Angels, Dean Chance was traded to the Minnesota Twins in 1967. He responded by leading the American League in starts (39), complete games (18) and innings pitched (283 2/3). The last time the Twins and Red Sox met (August 6, 1967), Chance and Jim Lonborg were on the mound. Chance pitched a five-inning rain-shortened perfect game and the Twins beat the Red Sox 2-0.

In the final two weeks of the '67 season, which team led the American League was a matter of which edition of the newspaper you read that day. With two weeks left to play, Minnesota, Detroit, Chicago and the Red Sox were all separated by one game—total. Percentage points, really.

Now our "Impossible Dream" season was coming to an impossible conclusion. The Red Sox were in a dead tie with the Minnesota Twins—and we were playing them at Fenway in the final game of the season.

I'd been in a zone, playing the best baseball I'd ever played, batting .523 with 5 home runs and 16 RBI in two weeks.

Boston Red Sox 0 : Minnesota Twins 2

Game played on Sunday, August 6, 1967, at Metropolitan Stadium

Boston Red Sox	ab	r	h	rbi	Minnesota Twins	ab	r	h	rbi
Andrews 2b	2	0	0	0	Versalles ss	2	0	0	0
Jones 3b	2	0	0	0	Tovar 2b	1	1	0	0
Yastrzemski 1f	2	0	0	0	Oliva rf	2	0	1	0
Conigliaro rf	2	0	0	0	Killebrew 1b	2	1	1	0
Siebern 1b	2	0	0	0	Allison 1f	2	0	1	1
Petrocelli ss	2	0	0	0	Rollins 3b	2	0	1	1
Smith cf	1	0	0	0	Uhlaender cf	2	0	0	0
Howard c	1	0	0	0	Zimmerman s	2	0	0	0
Lonborg p	1	0	0	0	Chance p	2	0	0	0
Totals	15	0	0	0	Totals	17	2	4	2

Boston	0	0	0	0	0 —	0	0	0
Minnesota	0	0	0	2	0 —	2	4	0

Boston Red Sox	IP	H	R	ER	BB	SO
Lonborg L (15-5)	4.1	4	2	2	1	7
Totals	4.1	4	2	2	1	7

Minnesota Twins	IP	H	R	ER	BB	SO
Chance W (14-8)	5.0	0	0	0	0	4
Totals	5.0	0	0	0	0	4

E-None 2B-Minnesota Oliva (20. off Lonborg): Allison (13. off Lonborg) SB-Tovar (13.2 nd base off Lonborg/Howard). U-Jim Odom, Hank Soar, Al Salemo, Ed Runge. T-2:11. A-26.003.

I'd just gone from game to game. I might have been aware of the pressure of the pennant, but I really didn't have time for it. Lying there in my hotel bed, though, with this one game to play, it all crashed down on me. Through the night my mind raced, every doubt and anxiety I hadn't felt during the stretch drive suddenly coming in on me, high and tight. My two-week high collapsed around me in the dark. I'd been playing like I was superhuman; now, when I needed it most, I felt very ordinary.

When I got back to Boston, I pushed my breakfast around my plate. Then I threw down my napkin and drove to Fenway. I should have gotten more sleep. This was the most important game of my life, and I felt tired, heavy, scattered and achey. After I got my uniform on and signed the usual collection of balls, bats and pictures, I tried taking some batting practice. What aspirin is to most people, batting practice was to me. I couldn't hit anything out of the infield, though. My swing felt tight. I just decided to try to stop thinking about the situation. Whatever I'd had this season, it had left me. Simple as that. Maybe I'd surprise myself this afternoon. But I doubted it.

I took my usual pregame nap and then a cold shower.

"What aspirin is to most people,
batting practice was to me."

FENWAY WAS STANDING ROOM ONLY.

Game time. Fenway was packed, electric. The Fenway Faithful were crazy with pennant fever. It would be the first one they'd gotten in 21 years—if we could win. If. I felt better after the nap and a fast leg rub, but I was still short of sleep. My stomach was complaining, my mind whirling.

I'd gotten a homer and four RBI against the Twins in the first game of the two-game series. But that was yesterday. Now nothing was right. I did my best at the plate, and collected a single and a double, but the bat felt heavy. And in left field, where I'd been able to feel like an All-Star even on off days at the plate, I was charged with an error and missed at least one other chance.

In the bottom of the sixth, the Red Sox were down by two runs. I was pacing like an animal in the dugout, trying to get something going, trying to find whatever I'd had the last two weeks.

Jim Lonborg, our pitcher, surprised the Twins with a bunt and beat out the throw to first. Jerry Adair moved him over to second with a single to center. Dalton Jones came to the plate. As I stepped into the batter's circle, the crowd noise was crossing the pain threshold.

Maybe it was the screaming and clapping. Maybe it was the desperate clutch situation, I don't know.

But the clouds parted.

My head was clear, my bat felt light and my aches were gone. I couldn't wait to step to the plate.

Jones showed bunt but then blooped one over Cesar Tovar's head into left. The bases were loaded.

I stepped into the batter's box. All the complaints, all the doubt were gone. I was right where I was supposed to be. It was as if my whole career, my whole life had led to this one moment.

I rubbed dirt on my hands and dug in. The noise was deafening. We'd probably all lose our minds if we listened to it long enough. But just then—though I saw the fans, the waving, the clapping—I didn't hear anything at all.

The bat, the stance, the grip, everything that was wrong was now right. Standing in, I could feel the power of my swing again. Dean Chance threw a fastball. I laid off it. Low and inside. Ball one.

I knew the pitch I was looking for. And I knew it was going to be the next one. It was: sinker low and away. As bad as I felt before the game, it couldn't have been more natural. I stepped into the pitch and rocketed it over second base for a two-RBI single. Game tied.

By the end of the inning it was 5-2. And Chance was gone.

But the game wasn't over yet. In the top of the eighth, Killebrew and Oliva each touched Lonborg for singles. Bob Allison came to the plate, the kind of right-handed hitter who eats Fenway's 315-foot left field for lunch.

Pull-hitting righties love the Wall. Hit it high enough and it's pretty easy to get it out. And where it meets the grandstand fence, back in the corner, where there's hardly any foul territory and no running room, is a spot you could call the Black Hole of Fenway: a spot so tough to fish a ball out of that it almost guarantees a double. With two men on and only a three-run cushion, we couldn't give them a double.

But that corner was just where Allison hit it on the next pitch.

I jumped to my right as soon as the ball left Allison's bat. It was a grounder burning its way along the foul line, but I got to it just in time and stabbed it with a backhand. I turned, off balance, I planted my foot against the grandstand wall. In an instant, without pausing, I scanned the infield. I wasn't going to get Killebrew, who was heading home. I could try for Oliva, who was rounding third, but the play at the plate would be close, too close. There was only one play. Rocking against my planted foot, I fired the ball in to Andrews at second, beating Allison under his hook slide and ending the inning. The Twins were held to one run.

Pure Fenway instinct.

One inning later, we won the game.

Crazed Sox fans jumped on starter Jim Lonborg as he tried to get back in the clubhouse and ripped his clothes to shreds.

We hadn't won the pennant—not yet, anyway. If the Tigers beat the Angels, there would be a play-off. But later that afternoon, the Angels won, giving the Sox sole possession of first place—and the pennant. This time it was the players who went mad. We doused each other with champagne, beer and shaving cream, hooting and hollering, hugging each other, dancing around, jumping on the tables. Everybody who had been part of our season was cramming into the clubhouse.

Then I caught sight of my dad in the back of the room. He had sacrificed so much to give me this moment. But now he was beaming. He looked fulfilled, as if he couldn't ask for anything more.

Our eyes locked. As the jets of champagne whizzed past, I was taken from that overheated locker room to the cold, rocky potato fields where my journey had begun. **8**

Minnesota Twins 3 : Boston Red Sox 5

Game played on Sunday, October 1, 1967, at Fenway Park

Minnesota Twins	ab	r	h	rbi	Boston Red Sox	ab	r	h	rbi
Versalles ss	3	0	0	0	Adair 2b	4	1	2	0
Reese ph, lf	1	0	1	0	Andrews 2b	0	0	0	0
Tovar 3h	3	1	0	0	Jones 3b	4	1	2	0
Killebrew 1b	2	2	2	0	Yastrzemski **lf**	4	1	4	2
Oliva rf	3	0	2	0	Harrelson lf	3	0	0	1
Allison lf	4	0	1	1	Tartabull pf, rf	1	1	0	0
Hemandez ss	0	0	0	0	Scott 1h	4	0	0	0
Uhlaender cf	4	0	1	0	Petrocelli ss	3	0	1	0
Carew 2b	4	0	0	0	Smith cf	4	0	0	1
Zimmerman c	2	0	0	0	Gibson c	2	0	0	0
Nixon ph, c	1	0	0	0	Siebern ph	1	0	0	0
Rollins ph	1	0	0	0	Howard c	1	0	1	0
Chance p	2	0	0	0	Lonborg p	4	1	2	0
Worthington p	0	0	0	0	Totals	35	5	12	4
Kostro ph	1	0	0	0					
Roland p	0	0	0	0					
Grant p	0	0	0	0					
Totals	31	3	7	1					

Minnesota	1	0	1	0	0	0	0	1	0	—	3	7	1
Boston	0	0	0	0	0	5	0	0	X	—	5	12	2

Minnesota Twins	IP	H	R	ER	BB	SO	Boston Red Sox	IP	H	R	ER	BB	SO
Chance L (20-14)	5.0	8	5	5	0	2	Lonborg W (22-9)	9.0	7	3	1	4	5
Worthington	1.0	0	0	0	1	1	Totals	9.0	7	3	1	4	5
Roland	00	3	0	0	0	0							
Grant	2.0	1	0	0	0	1							
Totals	8.0	12	5	5	1	4							

E-Killebrew (12), Yastrzemski (7), Scott (19), **DP**-Minnesota 3, Boston 2. **2B**-Minnesota Oliva (34. off Lonborg) Boston Yastrzemski (31, off Chance). **IBB**-Olive (12 by Lonborg). **WP**-Worthington 2 (5). **IBB**-Longborg (5, Olive). **U**-Nestor Chylak, Cal Drummond, Marty Springstead, Jim Honochick. **T**-2:25. **A**-35,770.

JIM LONBORG SHARES THE WIN AND HIS UNIFORM WITH RED SOX FANS.

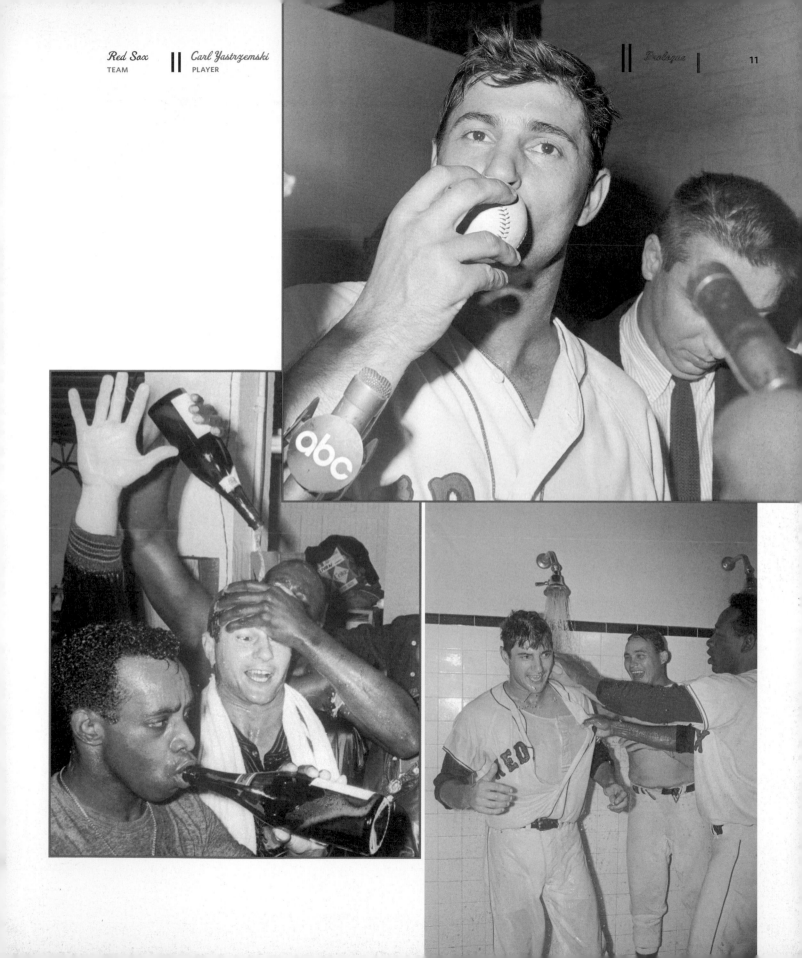

GIMMICKS IN THE GARAGE

The Making of a Baseball Player

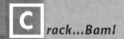

C *rack...Bam!*

The baseball on the string swung in a tight arc and smacked into the ceiling.

I breathed out a huge cloud of steam. Inside the heavy sheepskin coat, I adjusted my stance. The January wind blasted off the Atlantic and rattled the window of the garage while the ball dangled from its string. I tightened my grip around the heavy training bat.

Crack...Bam!

My swing was tight. The bulky gloves felt funny on the bat. And the coat wasn't helping me get around on the ball. But I had another hour out here. I'd warm up.

Bottom line was *Crack...Bam!* when I got back to the high school team next year *Crack...Bam!* I was going to do a lot more *Crack...Bam!* than bunt.

Crack...whup.

Oops. The ball stuck in the ceiling.

Well, I thought, climbing up onto the top of our old truck to pry it out, I guess I'm getting stronger.

I always knew I wanted to be a ballplayer. When you're little you don't have a plan all mapped out, complete with college ball, pro recruiting and stops in the minors. But playing big-league ball was all I thought about, like millions of other American boys in the '40s and '50s. Baseball was everything then. It was the golden age of DiMaggio, Mantle, Mays, Williams and Musial. For me, nothing could come close to playing at their level.

Most people have their dreams but wake up to a very different kind of life. You might say I was lucky to live my fantasy and end up in the Baseball Hall of Fame. And I have been fortunate—I've been blessed. But there was more to it than luck. A lot more. My baseball dreams powered daily hitting, throwing and drilling, and fuelled an obsession, a burning need from day one, to be the best.

Anyone who's going to play pro sports is going to need something like that kind of drive. It's not enough to want to play ball—you gotta *have* to play ball. That was me—living, sleeping, breathing, dreaming, eating baseball—day, night, summer, winter.

But right from the start, I faced a big challenge: I was small. A 120-lb. high school freshman, barely 5'9". A lot punier than the big juniors and seniors who were pitching me fireballs. It was going to take something extra for me to play baseball for a living.

I looked at my family. At all the other farmers pulling their livelihood out of the ground every year. Just like them, I knew I'd have to work at it that much harder to make it.

I never did get very big. Topped out at 5'11" and signed with the Red Sox at 160 lbs.

So I never stopped working at it.

Bridgehampton, near the tip of Long Island, was no playground for the rich in 1939. At least not the Bridgehampton I was born in. It was working folks hanging on as best they could. Immigrants, mostly, Italians and Irish—and lots of Polish farmers working potatoes in hard times, just like they had in the old country.

Potato farming is not an easy life. The days are long. The profits are thin. And hauling those things around can break your back. My dad, Carl Sr., had some land up the road from us in Water Mill that he farmed with his brother Tommy since before I came along.

They sacrificed a lot to make that farm go. Especially Dad. He probably could have played major league ball. He might have had a great career. But he wanted to make sure he could feed a family, and he thought farming was a more reliable, responsible way to do it.

Dad and Tommy were just hanging on some years. Eventually, they made a go of it. Because as bad as things got during the Great Depression, Americans always needed potatoes. Especially when they couldn't afford much else.

By the time I was growing up we were doing OK. OK as in I had a new coat every year. I always ate pretty well, too. Raising all your own food helps with that. We had a huge garden out back where we grew all our own vegetables. My grandparents raised and slaughtered livestock. We even churned our own butter. But even though I grew up in the more prosperous period after World War II when we probably could have afforded to just buy butter at the store, in a way the lean years of the Depression shaped my life.

My mom and dad had lived through tough times, years when the challenge of putting food on the table trumped everything else. They were all about living simply, knowing the value of a dollar and keeping focused on necessities. And they drummed that message into me.

"Ya gotta save! Put it in the bank!"

They taught me that life can throw you some tough curves, some no-hitters. Nothing is going to be handed to you.

But it wasn't just my parents' history that made me the player I was and the guy I am today; I'm a farm boy. Growing up on a farm taught me that if your dreams are going to come true, then you're going to have to build them with your own two hands. Those are really the only things you can count on.

I was using my hands to help out on the farm as soon as I could heft a bag of potatoes. Lazy days of summer? Mine began with a knock on the door at 5 a.m.

"Let's go," said Dad's voice.

I'd pull on my clothes, head into the potato fields and work there with Dad until sunset every day. Harvesting, moving irrigation pipes, sacking potatoes and loading trucks with the sacks was as hard as it sounds—harder, maybe, because most of this was before there were mechanical or automated ways of doing it. Those sacks were heavy. They helped my body get strong and hard.

They also showed me what my future could be like if I didn't make it in baseball. There was no rest for a farm boy in the winter, no matter how cold it got. We'd cut sprouts

out of the hundreds of old potatoes to plant in the spring. No automation there, either—we'd do it by hand, bending over our work, a potato in one hand and a knife in the other. On school days, I'd be expected to grab a knife and do my share when I got home.

Even though we worked hard and never had much money, life was abundant in one very important way, and that was family. There were Mom and Dad and my brother Rich and I, but my folks had all their close relatives nearby in Bridgehampton or Southampton, too. So I grew up in a world of cousins, aunts, uncles and grandparents. The Yastrzemskis and the Skoniecznys—my mom's folks—farmed together, ate together and played together. In a way, the greatest Red Sox teams I played for were an extension of that great family feeling.

MY AUNTS, JEAN SKONIECZNY HOINSKI AND REGINA SKONIECZNY FALKOWSKI, BAGGING POTATOES

THE TISKA FAMILY POTATO FARM WAS A DEAD RINGER FOR MY FATHER CARL SR.'S. TONY TISKA SR., SPANKY TISKA
AND TONY TISKA JR. WITH "GUMP" TISKA ON THE TRACTOR CIRCA 1944.

I was particularly close with Grandpa Skonieczny. He was kind of my surrogate father during the summer harvest seasons when I was still too small to help my parents with the potatoes. I would spend every day with him, helping tend his livestock, riding his tractor or crabbing at the shore. My memories of my grandparents are seasoned with delicious tastes: of freshly caught crab we'd boil up back at the farmhouse; the czarnina (duck soup), golompki (stuffed cabbage) and plum-potato dumplings that Grandma Skonieczny made; and the ice cream Grandpa Skonieczny used to buy me at the Candy Kitchen.

Even stronger than those tastes in my memory, though, are the sounds of baseball, the feel of a bat and the sight of a ball coming towards me. The game was woven into my childhood and my family like the red stitching around a ball.

My dad got me a little toy bat when I was just a baby. They tell me I dragged it around everywhere I went like a security blanket or a stuffed animal. By the time I was six my dad was pitching a tennis ball to me after supper in the backyard. That drill evolved into Yankees-Red Sox games, where I'd hit for every player in both lineups, switching right to left and changing my stance depending on whether I was supposed to be DiMaggio or Williams. My brother Rich joined in the game when he was old enough, and the game got more and more complex. Neighbors' yards and houses stood in for right, center and left, and different walls and garage doors meant doubles, triples, homers or outs. You know the way kids' games are.

Come to think of it, those rules might have helped prepare me for left field in Fenway. The Wall could make games a lot crazier and more arbitrary than anything I played with Rich.

Eventually I graduated from tennis balls to baseballs. My dad and I would go to the fairgrounds across the street and he'd throw me a bucket of fastballs, then go way out there to shag them. This went on for an hour or more, every night that it was light and warm enough. And it just seemed like the most natural thing in the world.

Dad was my coach, my first talent scout and my baseball buddy. He was a great shortstop who could hit for average and power, a guy who lived and breathed baseball same as I did. On Tuesday and Thursday nights Dad played shortstop with the Falcons, a legendary semipro team based in nearby Riverhead. He was one of the founders of our local team, the Bridgehampton White Eagles. The White Eagles were all Polish guys—mostly Yastrzemskis and Skoniecznys, in fact. They were like our family ball club. Technically, the

Red Sox
TEAM

Carl Yastrzemski
PLAYER

⃣0 ⃣1
CHAPTER NO.

19

White Eagles were just a spin-off from the Bridgehampton Polish-American social club that put on dances and other events, but all the money they made from dances went right into uniforms.

Dad hit well enough to get scouted by major league teams during the Depression. Times being uncertain as they were then, though, and a family on the way, he tried to forget about the major leagues and give his all to the potato farm. He never said so, but I know he hated having to do that. After I was born, he gave it one more shot and tried out with the Cardinals and the Dodgers. The Brooklyn Dodgers, that is. And the Dodgers offered him a contract—Class D, $75 a month.

(TOP) MY GRANDFATHER AND GRANDMOTHER'S WEDDING PICTURE FROM 1915
(BOTTOM) BIG MIKE AND EVA SKONIECZNY OUTSIDE THEIR FARM

There was no way he could make that work. He'd hurt his shoulder, he was already 23 with a wife and kid, and his prospects for getting to the majors were getting slimmer. He turned away from the majors and put his heart into semipro ball—and me.

Dad was still a passionate fan, though. Lived and died with the Yankees. And pretty soon, so did I. We'd drive down to Yankee Stadium four times a year to see Joe DiMaggio and Whitey Ford and Mickey Mantle, and then on the way back up to Bridgehampton we'd talk about the great plays we'd seen, or how they were doing in the pennant race. And of course we had our own "fantasy" Yankees team when he threw me batting practice. I liked the Red Sox, too, because they had left-hander Ted Williams, and the Cardinals, who won three World Series behind another great lefty, Stan "The Man" Musial. But the Yan-

THE BRIDGEHAMPTON WHITE EAGLES. FAR LEFT, KNEELING, IS MY DAD, CARL SR., AND I'M THE SQUIRT IN FRONT. JUST ABOUT EVERYONE ELSE HAS EITHER THE LAST NAME YASTRZEMSKI OR SKONIECZNY

kees were my guys. In fact, my baseball dreams weren't just about wanting to play in the majors. I wanted to be a Yankee.

In one way I was raised on a farm with a big, extended family that played a lot of baseball. Looking at it another way, though, you could almost say I was raised into a big, family baseball team that farmed potatoes in their spare time. Baseball was behind everything. After work, my dad would talk about the Yankees. In the fields, my cousins and I practiced our swings by hitting bushels of rocks. And the harvest season was also White Eagles season; on Sundays all the Yastrzemskis and Skoniecznys would vie for the championship against other teams in the Suffolk County League.

When I was ten years old I read about Paul Pettit, the first "bonus baby." He'd signed with the Pirates in 1951 for $100,000. That was a lot of money back then, as much as $1,000,000 or more in 2007 dollars. And you also have to consider that even All-Stars didn't get paid a lot in the '50s relative to what even an average player makes now. That kind of a signing bonus was wild, extraordinary, unheard of.

Pettit actually never amounted to much, and didn't pitch in the major leagues after 1953. I didn't know that at the time, of course—and it probably wouldn't have mattered. $100,000 was still a lot of money. Add all those zeros to a kid's obsession with baseball, his goal of getting off a potato farm and his dad's deferred dream, and you've got one powerful cocktail—just enough to give me a fever about playing pro ball for a living. (It gave Dad some ideas, too.)

So I started to get even more intense with my training.

I'd hit rocks out in the fields when we were laying irrigation pipe. Play imaginary All-Star games with my friend Tony Tiska (he played all the righties, me the lefties). Wash dishes for Billy DePetris—who eventually signed with the Giants—so I could drag him out of his dad's restaurant and try to hit his knuckleball.

I got my Uncle Mike Skonieczny to rig up a gadget for me, an adjustable contraption made out of iron pipe, rubber hose, 200 feet of string and a baseball, so I could whack the ball at the fairgrounds without shagging it, even when I was alone. Anything so I could hit—every day.

Or pitch, for that matter. Obsessed as I was with hitting, I had the idea for a few years that I would be more likely to make it as a pitcher. Even when I was six or seven, when you're just into stuff, rather than training for your career. I rigged up another kind of gimmick in the garage, a strike-zone-sized square I drew on the inside back wall. I'd stand outside the garage and throw a tennis ball at it 30 minutes at a time, just at one corner, ball after ball, getting it right.

I got into Little League as soon as I was old enough, and then Babe Ruth League, where I pitched, caught, played shortstop and just about every other position. My pitching practice paid off: I threw a no-hitter once. But my dad, who coached the team, was looking at the bigger picture. He could see I had the stuff and the drive to make it as a ballplayer, and he had me play shortstop as much as possible because he thought that was my natural position—the one I'd most likely end up in playing the majors.

That Babe Ruth team was great. We went to the state championship and won it all. I was at my peak—playing against other twelve-year-olds, that is. Joining the Bridgehampton high school team the next year was a big reality check.

I was good enough to make varsity as a freshman. Maybe that didn't mean a lot, small as Bridgehampton High was; there were 80 kids in the whole place. That didn't make the diamonds any smaller, though. Up to this point I'd been playing on Little League fields. Compared to regulation diamonds, they're, well, little. I played shortstop for Bridgehampton, and did OK because I had a strong arm, but hitting was another story. I just couldn't get the ball out of the infield. I wasn't big enough or strong enough. So I bunted.

I placed my bunts well and was fast enough to make it on base, so I was able to compile a decent batting average that way. But I was always a competitive guy, and I was just hitting adolescence, too. This approach wasn't doing much for my self-image. I mean, girls were watching!

I turned to my dad for help.

"I've been working on my hitting for a long time now," I said to him, kicking the ground. I felt like I was going to cry, I was so frustrated. "Do you mean to tell me I'm going to be a bunter all my life?! What can I do? There's gotta be something!"

"Listen, Carl," he said, trying not to smile, "you're a natural hitter. All that hitting you've been doing is paying off—your mechanics are real strong and your wrist action's good. Now, you're just thirteen. But that means you're going to be growing a lot next year. You'll be bigger and stronger, and you'll do better. If you want to do more, develop your shoulder and arm muscles, then work out with a lead bat over the winter."

He looked at me.

"But it's not going to be much fun."

He was right about that. Where we lived, the thermometer didn't poke above freezing much in the depths of winter—and that garage was unheated. But I knew he was right. It was what I had to do if I wanted to get to the next level.

Before winter set in I set myself up in the garage. I got myself a heavy training bat with a lead core, drove a nail through a ball and hung it from the ceiling. I'd already built some other gimmicks out of the pipes and hose we always had lying around; I brought them all in there and set them up so I could work my wrists, shoulders and arms, too. When the snow started to fall, I kept the path from the back door to the garage clear. An hour before supper I'd sprint out there in my bulky coat and start swinging that bat.

I'd swing it 1,000 times. Every night.

GRAMMAR SCHOOL—THAT'S ME THIRD FROM THE LEFT, STANDING

My mom would eventually call me in to eat, but then I'd hustle back out there for another hour, doing muscle-specific drills.

Tell you what, it paid off. The workouts, combined with my natural growth over the winter, made me a completely different batter. I tore up our high school league. And I continued to do it in my junior and senior years, too, hitting .650 in my senior season, and winning the Suffolk County Class B championship while pitching a no-hitter.

Baseball was my game—there was never any question about that. But I loved all sports. When I tried out for the basketball team as a shrimpy 5'9" freshman, the coach drew me aside.

"Son," he said, "you've got a lot of athletic ability. But let's face it, you're a little small. You're not the fastest guy in the world, either. Still, you've got a good eye and good arms. I think you could be a scoring threat from the outside. Why don't you work on that? Maybe you could get a peach basket and hang it up in your backyard or something."

So that's exactly what I did. It was just like swinging the lead bat or pitching to the back of the garage. I dunked three-pointers into that peach basket every chance I got—over and over and over again. I even shoveled the driveway so I could practice through the winter.

HIGH SCHOOL—SECOND FROM THE RIGHT, SITTING

Pretty soon I was unstoppable from three-point range—or at least I would have been if we'd had three-pointers back then! It seemed like no matter how far outside defenses pushed me, I could still make shots. And I could drive and jump, and eventually I showed a lot of quickness inside, too. The 628 points I scored on our basketball team in the 1956-57 season is still a Suffolk County record. Again, I developed a game that suited my size by working on it, and working on it, and working on it.

I liked football, too. I got in some time as quarterback on our six-man team, but my dad wasn't having any of that. He'd told me not to play football. When I did it anyway he stormed onto the field and practically stripped my shoulder pads off. He was furious.

"You're not going to break no collarbone playing football!"

He was going to make sure I didn't miss a single opportunity that my ability and passion created for me. That's why Dad blew his top when he saw me with the helmet and pads. He could see a successful major league career wiped out by a single tackle.

As a kid I wasn't really aware how, pretty much from the start, he'd been planning my whole career. Dad wasn't a big talker. Like a lot of guys of his generation, men who'd seen hardship and sacrificed a lot, he tended to hold things in. So when he'd step up and push me back onto the path he felt I should be on, it surprised me.

I feel like I ought to add this: while Dad had some firm ideas about the best choices for me as I started out my career, he was not one of these types who push and micromanage their kids to make themselves look better. My dad understood and accepted who he was. He was mighty proud of me, but he was proud of his farm, too. And he played a heck of a lot of baseball and was one of the greatest hitters I ever saw. Dad packed a lot of life into his years. He didn't need to live through me.

I guess you could say I broke into professional baseball with the Riverhead Falcons. I was their batboy. But it was the Bridgehampton White Eagles that gave me my first experience playing in the pros. If you wanted to call it the pros.

I joined the team in 1954, when I was 14. I played center field. My Uncle Jerry was in left, Uncle Mike was in right, Uncle Ray played third, Uncle Stosh caught and Uncle Chet, with his creaky, complaining arm, did most of our pitching. The rest of the team was filled out by cousins and a few friends. Dad played shortstop, managed and kept the team alive when his aging brothers and brothers-in-law would have preferred to call it a career.

Charles Forte, Huntington   Alvin Marquis, Amityville   Ron Bartlett, Amityville   Dick Breese, Greenport   Carl Yastrzemski, Bridgies

All-Scholastic '5' Has Height, Class

Cream of County's Court Stars

By Charles Clark

The answer to a coach's prayer—a team averaging 6-1 in height and possessed of great speed, rebounding strength and tremendous scoring potential—that's the Newsday All Scholastic basketball team, which boasts only one holdover from last season.

This year, Newsday's All - Scholastic represents the top five players in Suffolk County. Based on eye-witness reports, statistics, discussions with coaches and officials during the season, the top players have merited positions on the stellar quintet by virtue of their all-around value, not merely on the basis of scoring records.

At the helm of this mythical county team Newsday puts Merle Wiggins, Bridgehampton's championship producer. What havoc this team could wreak in scholastic cage circles can only be imagined, but such a mixture of experience and youthful enthusiasm would be hard to beat.

the jump-shot wizard was almost a sure bet to do it. Unfortunately, in the heat of battle, no one gave any thought to records.

Marquis was one of the big reasons for the success of Amityville and his talent with the very soft flip was such that opposing teams frequently double-teamed the speedy lad, but to little avail.

Ron Bartlett, Marquis' 6-3 senior teammate, didn't get as many headlines, but among the sporting fraternity members, he was the big man on the Tide team. Devoid of Marquis' flashy, crowd-pleasing style, Bartlett was a tower of strength in the rebound department under both boards, and many of his points came via tap-ins.

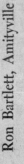

Name	School	Age	Hgt.	Class	Yrs. Varsity
Alvin Marquis	Amityville	18	6-3	Sr.	3
Charles Forte	Huntington	17	6-0	Sr.	3
Dick Breese	Greenport	17	6-2	Jr.	2
Carl Yastrzemski	Bridgehampton	16	5-10	Jr.	3
Ron Bartlett	Amityville	17	6-3	Sr.	3

HONORARY COACH: Merle Wiggins, Bridgehampton High School.

Wiggins Popular Choice For 'Coach of Year' Title

The old saying "It couldn't have happened to a nicer guy" may be a bit shop-worn by now, but it remains more than appropriate in the case of Merle Wiggins of Bridgehampton—Newsday's selection as the 1955-56 Basketball Coach of the Year.

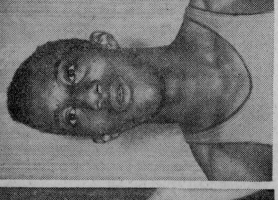

basketball Coach of the Year.

This latest honor comes to Wiggins when he is literally sitting on top of the scholastic sports world. His basketballers recently annexed their third straight B-3 League title and their first County Class B championship. Earlier in 1955, Wiggins coached the Bridgie baseball team to the County Class B crown.

The small, bespectacled man, who has had phenomenal success at the tiny Bridgehampton school, is one of the best liked and most respected personalities in Suffolk's sports picture. His teams, despite their usually small size, have always been held in high esteem by their opponents.

Wiggins came to the Eastern Suffolk school in 1942 after a coaching career that includes stops at Henderson High (NY), Springfield College and Portsmouth, N.H. While at Dover High in New Hampshire, Wiggins gained the unique distinction of being captain of four sports teams during his senior year.

Football, baseball, basketball and track were Wiggins' specialties at Dover and he continued the quartet of activities while at Springfield College. At Bridgehampton High, Wiggins has coached baseball, basketball and six-man football and added a third championship during his great 1955-56 year by taking the six-man title for a second straight campaign.

This year's Bridgie team was typical of Wiggins-coached squads—well drilled in fundamentals, lots of spirit and extreme coolness under fire. Most of his opponents say that "you might out-size Bridgehampton teams, but you have to go some to out-hustle them."

Now approaching 45 years of age, Wiggins' background includes several years of semi-pro baseball and basketball. He is married and an avid sports fan. A firm believer in scouting any and all teams, Wiggins is a familiar sight at any important ball game. He probably figures that sooner or later, his teams may have to tangle with one of the squads involved and he might as well have a line on them.

to beat.

Statistically, the lone repeater on the All-Scholastic is Huntington's great performer—Charlie Forte. A six-foot, fleet-footed ball hawk, Forte is acknowledged to be without a peer as a backcourt man and field general. Forte, who also gained a spot on the Newsday All-Scholastic football team, carried some of his gridiron talents over the basketball floor where he was a tireless driver and a constant harasser on defense.

Forte Lone Holdover

In the A-1 loop, Forte dunked 175 points, fourth high in that league. His big value to coach John Sipos, whose Blue Devils won two County Class A championships before losing to Amityville in a league playoff this year, was his team spirit. In addition to his varied talents, Forte has exemplified the spirit of sportsmanship during his career at Huntington.

Coach Jack Schmitt's Crimson Tide cagers, who won the County Class A crown this season, have two men on the Suffolk Top Five — the only school to place more than one man. It only illustrates the wealth of talent that Amityville had this year.

Alvin Marquis, a 6-3 senior, was second best public high scorer in Suffolk with 455 points. He missed a new county one-game high when he sat out a fourth period against Bay Shore after scoring 46 markers to that point. With only six points needed to establish a new standard,

A spot on the Top Five squad must be reserved for Greenport's superlative scoring ace, Dick Breese, who was number one in Suffolk with 459 points. One of the two juniors on the All-Scholastic, Breese was a big reason why the Oyster-men tied for the B-2 lead before losing to Mattituck in a loop playoff battle.

Standing 6-2, Breese is the latest in a long line of Breese boys, all of whom were standout athletes at Greeport High. A fine clutch player with a variety of shots, Breese was a full-time performer because of his defensive ability.

That leaves the number five spot open for another junior and the smallest man on the squad — Carl Yastrzemski of Bridgehampton. Only 5-10, Yastrzemski, whose baseball talents have tabbed him a good bet to make the major leagues, is no less a figure on the basketball floor.

Yastrzemski led the B-3 loop with 300 points, enough to net him tenth place in the Suffolk point tally. A fine playmaker who can thread the needle with passes, Yastrzemski personified the spirit of the always-smaller, but never-out-hustled Bridgies.

That's it! Newsday's All-Scholastic Five. While the selection of these five players was extremely difficult because of the large number of standout cagers playing in Suffolk this season, the facts and figures point, undeniably, to Marquis, Forte, Breese, Yastrzemski and Bartlett as the best in the county. As for Wiggins, the record speaks for itself.

Seven-Game League Schedule Approved by Football Schools

Patchogue—The controversial league football set-up in Suffolk was settled on amicable terms last night with both A-1 and A-2 leagues agreeing to a seven-game league slate except Smithtown and Westhampton.

The two schools gave different reasons for not preferring a seven-game schedule. Thad Mularz of Smithtown stated his school lacked football personnel for a full-season schedule while Westhampton cited low enrollment, the smallest of all competing football schools.

However, both schools will be penalized under the new scoring system by the county's efficient chairman Cliff Latney. It gives two points for winning a game and one point for a tie. There will be no playoff between the two leagues or playoff to break tie.

The touchy football officials' plight was handled very equitably, with six varsity officials rated unsatisfactory in a field of more than 30. Those six were relegated to jayvee assignments. Four other officials, who worked jayvee games mainly, were also rated unsatisfactory. All will be notified as to their status by the chairman.

The football coaches approved seven teams of three officials to work games rather than the past year's rotating system. The possibility of a fourth official, who would act as timer, was tabled for study by the SCPHSAA.

Braun Stars Play Vets Tonight

Riverhead—The Carl Braun All-Stars launch their Suffolk debut tonight, tackling the Westhampton Vets, winners of the East End club basketball championship, in the Riverhead High School gym.

Braun has signed Gene Shue, Dick McGuire, Al McGuire, Connie Simmons and Sayville's Bill Thieben for this benefit fray, in which proceeds will go to the Riverhead Auxiliary Police Fund and the Riverhead Varsity Club.

Last year the Braun Stars swept all Suffolk opposition in giving fans a glimpse of some Knickerbocker cagers. The game will also mark Thieben's debut with a pro club.

21 e

Playing outfield was hell. Most of our games were in open potato fields. Meaning there were no walls or fences. You had to play deep, real deep, if you wanted to prevent home runs. We played so deep routine fly balls went for singles, doubles and even triples. We were just too far out to catch them. As the game went on, teams would get more hits because outfielders would be exhausted from running around so much.

I did OK my first year, even though at 14 I was probably the youngest guy ever to play semipro ball. In the summer of 1955 I started to hit my stride. I was pulling the ball pretty well, launching shots to the potato lot in right. I ended up with more and more homers as the potato plants grew over the summer and made it harder and harder to find the ball. It helped that I wasn't wasting energy running around in center. I'd moved to the infield, playing my natural position at shortstop. Dad went over to third to make room for me, and Uncle Ray was just as happy to go to the beach. We'd brought in some fresh blood, younger guys from my high school team, and we were pretty good that year.

Dad played second when his cousin Alex Borkowski wasn't available, and we both got a kick out of turning the double play. I batted third and Dad batted cleanup. Like I said, Dad was a great batter, hitting around .450, year in and year out. He hit some fearsome shots in those endless, open fields we played in. Then there was the time we hit back-to-back home runs against the Riverhead team. I'd just sent one over the center-right fence when Dad, a righty, blasted one about 450 feet out in left.

Between Bridgehampton High and the White Eagles, I was starting to get noticed. In fact, by my second year playing semipro, Bots Nekola, a Red Sox scout, had been following me for two years. The Sox farm director, John Murphy, wanted to know how I was doing.

"How's Yastrzemski doing?"
"Great! He's hitting .460 and his old man's hitting .480!"

"Hey, Bots," said Murphy, "are you sure you're watching the right Yastrzemski?"

Anyone could see Dad was holding the White Eagles together with athletic tape and willpower. It was getting harder and harder to round up all those uncles and cousins every Sunday. When they'd started the team, all the guys were a lot younger, still full of competitive fire. Now they were in their forties, farmers who were getting tired of spending their one day off fixing up the overgrown high school field for home games, or chasing baseballs through someone else's potato field. Dad's sheer stubbornness is what kept the White Eagles flying as long as they did.

He didn't talk much about it, but it was pretty clear that Dad was keeping the family team alive for me—so I could get more game experience during the summer and, mostly, so we could play together during the few years it was going to be possible.

The whole Eastern Suffolk County League ended up falling apart in 1956, my third year with the team. The White Eagles must not have been the only team suffering from semipro fatigue.

Dad and I had to drive to Lake Ronkonkoma, 60 miles away, to keep playing ball. The Lake Ronkonkoma Cardinals were a good team in a more serious league. We played three games a week and they paid their player. $20 a game, plus expenses. It wasn't much, but then we weren't doing it for the money. (Even though Dad was making more than he would have with the Dodgers.)

Those guys were mostly in their thirties, old enough to have more experience and power than me, young enough not to be creaky and cranky like the White Eagles. The drive down there was a pain, but the caliber of play was higher than anything else I'd faced. I'd be talking to myself between every pitch, making constant corrections to my stance, my swing, my timing. Analyzing every facet of the game—chewing on it the same way I would in the majors. I never did well enough to meet my expectations.

The last year Dad and I played together was 1958, the summer I came home from my first year at Notre Dame. I was 18—and Dad was 41. We were still the heart of the lineup with Lake Ronkonkoma, still turning the double play. I could tell he was getting tired, though. Playing third base and just getting to and from the games was taking more and more energy. But he never complained. Maybe he just took it out on the ball. He batted .410 that year—outhitting me by about 35 points.

By the time I got to be a senior in high school, the scouts were coming out of the woodwork like termites. It was time to start thinking seriously about my future in baseball.

And the future I could see wore pinstripes. 8

PLAN FOR THE BEST, PREPARE FOR THE WORST

Dad Calls the Shots

I slipped into the pants and buttoned up the flannel jersey with the N and the Y crossing over the left side of my chest. All the pinstripes moved with me as I bent over to pull on my cleats. I adjusted the blue cap on my head, grabbed my bat and glove and crossed the clubhouse.

Mickey Mantle and Whitey Ford were standing over by the trainer's room in their T-shirts, sharing a joke. And there was Tony Kubek, who was on his way to winning AL Rookie of the Year, talking with Hank Bauer and Bill Skowron. And wasn't that Yogi Berra over there?

"Hey, Carl?"

This wasn't any time to daydream. I really was making my way through the Yankee's big, spacious clubhouse, a place I'd imagined dressing in for as long as I could remember.

It wasn't exactly a fantasy visit, though. Nobody said a word to me. There wasn't a Yankee who gave me a second glance. Not even the batboys had taken any notice of me.

Here I would have given my right arm to be able to shake the Mick's hand, or maybe get Don Larsen's autograph, and I wasn't supposed to even talk to any of them. The fact of the matter was that as a high school kid, I shouldn't even have been there.

"Carl?"

"OK, Mr. Garland, I'm coming." Ray Garland, who scouted New York and Long Island for the Yankees, was waiting for me at the door. He led me through the runway and into the Yankees' dugout.

A middle-aged guy in a #2 uniform stood at the top of the steps. I recognized him right away: Frank Crosetti, who'd played shortstop with DiMaggio, Gehrig and all of those guys.

"Crow, Carl here is going to do some hitting, OK?" said Garland.

Crosetti had been with the team for 32 years, and had a face that had seen it all. I was just another skinny young guy hoping to make the Show.

"Yeah, all right. Come on, kid."

Crosetti turned his back on me and walked over to the batting cage. I followed him and soaked in the feeling. I'd been coming to the House that Ruth Built since I was little, but this was the first time I'd ever been on the field, where Ruth called his shot, Gehrig told the fans he was the luckiest guy in the world, DiMaggio built his record hitting streak and so many Series had been won. It was awesome. 457 feet to left-center. But—and this was the best thing about the place, as far as I was concerned—only 296 short feet to the right porch. It was that dimension that was going to put me up there with Ruth and Mantle—I just knew it.

"The kid goes in next," Crosetti said.

I swung my bat a few times to warm up. When the cage was empty, I stepped in. I felt good, loose. Right away I started my patter. "Gotta be quick," I was muttering to myself. "But don't jump too hard on it. Stay loose, now."

The practice pitcher threw me a nice fastball, right down the middle, and I lined it to center. A couple of pitches later I parked one in the empty right field seats. Then the pitcher—I don't know who he was, but he was on my side—warned me that he'd be throwing a curve. I hit that one out, too. Everything was clicking. By the tenth pitch, I'd hit four home runs, and Crosetti cut off the BP. I figured they wanted me to show them what I could do in the field, so I ran out with my glove, but Crosetti called me back.

"That's it, kid—you're done. Go in and get dressed."

Lee MacPhail wanted to see me. MacPhail was the Yankees' director of player

personnel. I met my dad, who'd been watching my tryout from the stands, and MacPhail greeted us, shook hands and sat us down in his office. He put his hands together on his desk and smiled at me.

"Carl," he said, "would you like to play for the Yankees?"

If there was one thing in the world that I ever wanted to do, that was it! I wanted to jump out of my chair, yell, sign anything he put in front of me. I was ready to move into Yankee Stadium right then and there. But I just said, "Uh, sure."

"We think you've got what it takes to play here. You'd start on one of our farm clubs, but then you'd be back here in no time."

A TYPICAL MICKEY MANTLE HOME RUN AT YANKEE STADIUM IN RIGHT FIELD.
THE 296- FOOT POLE LINE WAS A FEAST FOR MY YOUNG EYES.

He looked at Dad. "We'll give Carl $40,000 to sign with us."

Yes! It was all coming together. The majors, the Yankees, the stadium—and now, real money! This was the first time anyone had made us an offer. $40,000 was a heck of a lot of money, especially for potato farmers. It was more than the farm was worth—more than Dad's life savings, more than we'd ever seen in our lives. And it was being offered to us by the New York Yankees.

But when I looked over at Dad his arms were crossed and his jaw was set. I knew that look. My heart sank.

"Mr. MacPhail, it's going to take a lot more than that."

Ever since my second year of high school, when I started to tear up the Suffolk County division, the scouts had been watching me. They were easy to spot in the stands, guys in fedoras who scribbled in notepads instead of rooting for anybody. We got to know Bots Nekola pretty well. We met scouts from other organizations, too.

It was always informal; I hadn't even graduated from high school. But we knew the conversations were going to get more serious. My pitching and hitting were two of the main reasons why Bridgehampton had beat much bigger schools for the county championship. Then, in a New York City-Long Island high-school all-star game, I pitched three shutout innings, made some great plays at shortstop and then hit a 400-foot home run. There was a definite buzz around this Yastrzemski kid. Now we needed a game plan.

We knew major league clubs would be talking in a language we didn't understand—throwing around big figures and clauses and incentives—and using hardball negotiation tactics, too. We needed some help. And that's where Father Joe came in.

For a priest, Father Joe Ratkowski threw a nasty curveball. He'd been a great ballplayer in his youth, a major league prospect like Dad. He chose a life in the Church instead of one in baseball and ended up becoming our local parish priest. He was still a huge fan of the game, though, and kept his Sunday sermons short during the summer so the White Eagles could play on time. Father Joe was the one who really taught me how to pitch when I was young. He could see pretty early on that I had the drive and the talent to play the game well.

Father Joe came to Bridgehampton from Brooklyn, a borough about as wrapped up in its sports team as Green Bay is with the Packers. He got to be pretty close to some of the Dodgers players and front office people and knew the business end of the game.

My dad, a devout Catholic, sought Father Joe's advice on any number of personal and business matters. He had an insider's perspective and knew how to negotiate contracts, so he was also our trusted advisor when it came to my career. Well, he was my dad's trusted advisor. Not that I didn't trust Father Joe—I just didn't have much say in the matter. It may have been my life to live, but at that point the career decisions were Dad's to make.

"$100,000," Father Joe told my dad. "Don't take a penny less. He's worth it—we both know it, and they know it, too."

Dad liked hearing that. But he wanted even more. I was going to college—Dad had already decided that. He'd never had the chance, but he wanted to make sure that whatever happened with a baseball career I would have the job prospects that came with a college degree. And as he pointed out, college baseball programs were the equivalent of Class B ball—with an education attached. So the team that got me would be the team that was going to pay a six-figure bonus plus my college tuition—no matter how long it took me to finish my degree.

I was kind of scared by all those numbers. I thought about Paul Pettit, who'd broken the $100,000 barrier. He basically turned out to be a dud. So clubs were probably going to be careful about throwing money at an unproven kid just out of high school. What if teams balked at my dad's demands? Was I going to end up missing my chance to play on a team I liked?

It was the day after I won the county championship that the Yankees called and invited me down to work out in the Bronx. We'd get a chance to test our strategy.

Our meeting in MacPhail's office after the tryout had ended with both Dad and the Yankees agreeing to think about it. Dad took the time to tell Father Joe about the Yankees' offer. But Father Joe's advice was the same.

"Don't take 40, Carl," he told my dad. "Don't even take 80. He's worth six figures. Don't settle for less."

Two days later Ray Garland drove up to our house. After making sure my stickball buddies knew who he was and why he was there, I ran over from the fairgrounds.

As we all sat in our living room, Garland spent about ten minutes smooth-talking my dad. He went on with his patter about the history of the Yankees, the winning tradition, the virtual guarantee of World Series money, the salaries they paid their veterans and stars, the endorsements and promotional deals. All the while he revised his offer on a scratch pad he'd laid on the coffee table. He scribbled bigger and bigger numbers as he kept up the pitch.

Dad just looked at him like a stone statue.

Garland had started at $45,000—$5,000 more than the Yankees' initial offer from a few weeks before. He worked his way up from there, but he was also building castles in the air: the potential package, once I became the next DiMaggio and the postseason bonuses and advertising money started pouring in, was at a quarter million dollars.

My dad kept looking at him, and didn't say a thing. Dad was a farmer, a very practical guy. The only money in the here and now was the signing bonus.

And the Yankees still weren't offering nearly enough.

"Well, Carl," he said to my dad, "what do you think?"

Still the blank stare. Garland was beginning to get just a little uncomfortable, I think. He tried to play it cool. He'd just never faced anyone like my dad before.

"Look, Carl, I'll write down our top offer on this piece of paper," he said, ripping one off, "and you write your figure on this one." He ripped off another and slid it to my dad.

They both scribbled. My dad wrote his in big block numerals.

"100,000? Are you out of your mind?!" Garland snorted, his mouth just hanging open.

"No one on the Yankees ever got a bonus like that—and these guys are the greatest players in baseball! They're never going to pay you that much!!"

Garland slumped back in his chair, rolled his eyes and flipped his pencil way up in the air. He looked beaten.

He didn't know the half of it.

"All right, mister," my dad roared at Garland, jumping out of his chair, the veins standing out on his forehead. "You've got a lot of nerve coming into my house, calling me crazy and throwing pencils around! You just take all that junk, get out of here and never come back!!"

And that's just what Ray Garland did. When he walked out of our door, my hopes of playing for the Yankees—and the $60,000—walked out with him. Dad never spoke to the Yankees again, either—though they tried plenty of times.

Dad had to be tough and stubborn to survive in a hard business. I respected him for that. I knew that it was keeping the farm going, which meant putting food on our table and into my mouth. But it was frustrating to have him be so intractable where my career was concerned. As grateful as I am to my dad now for working with me, training me and making choices that worked out pretty darn well, there were times in my life that I was really angry at him for being so strict about what he thought was good for me.

With the Yankees definitely out of the picture, we started looking more seriously at college. I got good grades at Bridgehampton High and was president of my class (which had eighteen people in it). I had a tall pile of scholarship offers. Some were basketball scholarships from places like Duke, Miami, Florida—warm-weather sports powerhouses with strong baseball programs where I could practice almost year-round. The scholarship packages rivaled what the Yankees were offering, too. They included not only the tuition but spending money, a new wardrobe, a private apartment and a car. Stuff that would definitely raise eyebrows in today's NCAA.

Those offers sounded real good to me. But Dad had other ideas.

"Son, I think Notre Dame's a good school for you. They've got a great baseball program."

Notre *Dame?* A great *baseball* program?

Like a lot of people, Dad was a big Fighting Irish fan when it came to football. But he must have brainwashed himself into thinking he'd ever heard anything about their baseball program. It was when Father Joe talked up Notre Dame, and said he thought he could get me a baseball scholarship, that suddenly it became a great baseball school.

I couldn't see it. I was Catholic, still am, no question about that, but I didn't see what advantage there could be in getting a Catholic education in snowy Indiana when I could be in Florida taking batting practice on a fat scholarship. I tried to argue the point, but Dad had his mind made up. I might as well have been talking to a brick wall. He was dead set on my going to a Catholic school.

Scouts were clustered like flies at our Lake Ronkonkoma games that summer. But we didn't get any more real offers. So, with my acceptance to Notre Dame on a half basketball and half baseball scholarship, I headed off to South Bend in the fall.

It wasn't an easy transition. My life in Bridgehampton revolved around sports. At Notre Dame, though, freshmen weren't eligible. In any sport. They had freshman teams, but we didn't do anything more than scrimmage. After being the star of my high school baseball and basketball teams, batting third on two semipro teams and being scouted by the Yankees, I felt like a caged animal. It didn't help that the general managers of several major league teams had somehow gotten my telephone number on campus and were calling me on a regular basis.

In the same way, the regimentation at Notre Dame was a shock. They ran you around between classes and three-hour basketball practices and then shut the dorm lights off at 10 p.m. And not just the lights—the electricity. I was caught studying by flashlight under my covers, so I had to get up at 4 a.m. to serve Mass the rest of the semester.

I struggled at first, flunking one of my classes. I also lost Grandpa Skonieczny, my great friend from childhood, only a few weeks after I got to campus. He had elected to undergo risky brain surgery for the Parkinson's disease that was taking over his body. He didn't recover from the operation.

I felt like leaving South Bend more than a few times. I was fortunate to make some good friends, and counselors like Father Glenn Boarman—who listened to me, talked with me and gave me enough inspiration to come back for spring semester.

Things picked up at the end of the year. I got a chance to at least take batting practice, adjusted to the schedule and their brand of discipline and made dean's list. But I was still just biding time, I felt, until I could really start talking with major league teams about my future.

I didn't have long to wait.

Shortly after I got back home for the summer, an all-star doubleheader was put together so major league personnel could get a look at all the great Long Island prospects in one shot, young men who'd mostly been in high school the year before but were now "fair game." We weren't playing for league standings. No championship was riding on the line. But playing before all these scouts, farm system directors and GMs, it might have been the most important doubleheader I'd played in my young life. Then, just like pennant

GOODBYE YANKEES, HELLO NOTRE DAME.

races ten or twenty years later, I played best when it mattered.

In eight at bats that afternoon I collected seven hits, three of them for home runs. I also had a great day at shortstop, fielding every chance perfectly.

The phone started ringing off the hook. Crowds got noticeably bigger at Lake Ronkonkoma. Lots of people came to visit us out at the house.

I was in the spotlight. But Dad was directing the show.

The Braves, who played in Milwaukee then, were one of the first to approach us that summer. They sent their pitching coach to talk to us along with a scout...and they struck out. First, they weren't offering us any more than the Yankees did. Second, they wanted me as a pitcher. My dad told the Braves (nicely) that even if the money were right, which it wasn't, I wouldn't be pitching in the majors. He didn't want me hurting my arm. I was going to be a slugger.

Oh, thanks for letting me know, Dad. Dad was so set in his master plan for my career that he didn't really feel a need to talk with me about it. Like, this was the first time I'd heard I wasn't on the market as a pitcher. He'd always been all right with my pitching before; it made me a more complete ballplayer and helped me understand hitting. I guess that changed.

ONE OF THE FEW DAYS WARM ENOUGH FOR PRACTICE

After that, the Giants and Dodgers went to bat for me but struck out against Dad. He didn't want me on the West Coast.

With the Reds, the Red Sox and the Tigers also talking us up informally, the Phillies actually invited me to come down for a tryout. I had a great session down there, hitting them out of the park in every direction, and they offered me $95,000 and a chance to start with the Phillies that night. Plus, their owner, Bob Carpenter, even offered to pay my way at the University of Delaware.

But Dad pulled another demand out of his hat—that Carpenter should pay me $10,000 if I didn't finish college. Carpenter couldn't handle that one, and watched it sail right past him. Strike three.

As we left the park, Carpenter reminded us that his offer was open if Dad would rethink his last demand. He gave me his phone card number, told me to call anytime.

Bots Nekola of the Red Sox called when we got back to Long Island, finally inviting me down to Fenway for a tryout—but I was just about to leave for South Bend the next day. We set up a visit to Boston during the Thanksgiving vacation.

Cincinnati and Detroit also called with invitations to tryouts while I was back at Notre Dame. My dad picked me up at the beginning of break and we headed out to see all of them. Was I excited? Here I was, on my way to try out with three great ball clubs, one of which was going to sign me to play professional baseball for a fat, six-figure bonus. I was about to begin a career in the major leagues. You bet I was excited.

I loved Briggs Stadium (now called Tiger Stadium and scheduled for demolition in 2007). In fact, I ended up hitting more home runs there than any other park in the league, except Fenway. But Detroit couldn't go beyond $80,000 on the bonus, so they were out. Then Dad asked for $150,000 from the Cincinnati Reds, and they came up to $125,000— $125,000! For me!—but nope, Dad told their owner, it wasn't enough. Out!

Did Dad even want to sign with any of these clubs? He was coming up with stuff to kill every deal. Why? Near as I could figure, it was like this: my dad was a great farmer, but his potatoes weren't any better than anyone else's. All he could get for them was the market price, which wasn't very much. Now he was offering a precious commodity indeed: Carl Yastrzemski, Jr. There was only one of those. It was a seller's market. And gosh, he enjoyed setting the price. He was sticking it to these bigwigs and flexing some power for once.

Right Field At Fenway Measures 380 Feet, But Seems A Million Miles Away Compared To Yankee Stadium.

But in the meantime, I was afraid we were pricing ourselves right out of the market. It looked like I might run out of clubs that we could negotiate with. Being a potato farmer wasn't something I'd been thinking about lately, but maybe that was my destiny after all…

Well, there was just one batter left in this "inning," and that was the Red Sox. As we drove into Boston, I was just hoping Dad wouldn't throw 'em a spitter. Next to the Yankees, the Sox were my favorite team. Boston wasn't all that far away from us on Long Island. They had Ted Williams, the greatest left-handed slugger in baseball.

On the other hand, I had never seen Fenway before.

A little while later we were standing behind home plate. A field of snow lay between us and the right field seats, 380 feet away. There was so much wrong with the picture I didn't know where to begin.

Huh?

And that's when my dad said it:

"Carl, this is a great place for you to hit!"

The right field seats were so far away I could hardly even see them. Forget hitting homers out there. I'd also told Dad that one of the reasons I didn't get to work much on baseball at Notre Dame was because of the endless winters. Here at Fenway it wasn't even Thanksgiving and they were already having a white Christmas.

Dad didn't seem to notice that I was not very enthusiastic about the situation. He and Murphy were chatting and joking as we went up to the office. I noticed Dad didn't have his usual poker face on. The negotiations started and Dad came out with $125,000. A lot less than he'd asked of Cincy. But this time I thought, *why couldn't he have asked for more?* Maybe they'd just tell us to go away! The negotiations dragged on. Tom Yawkey, the owner of the Red Sox, called from his winter home in South Carolina and told us to sleep on it.

Dad and I had a heart-to-heart that night at the hotel. I told him why I thought Fenway was the wrong park for me. How maybe the Phillies or just about any other club would be a better fit. He countered my every argument pretty reasonably. It started to get late, though, and Dad was getting tired. I wasn't giving in, either. So he gave me an ultimatum: "Carl, you'll sign with the Red Sox or you'll go back to Notre Dame."

Wow, I thought as I lay back on the pillow. Boston is the only club Dad wants me to play for. I think he's had his mind made up from the start. But why? Well, it's close, but… ahhh! Father Joe! I remembered that Father Joe had spoken of the importance of a caring owner who knew his players and had a hand in negotiations. And he had singled out Mr. Yawkey. I bet there's a connection with the Church there somewhere. It's Notre Dame all over again, I thought, as I drifted off into a nightmare about an endless, snowy right field.

(I found out later that Tom Yawkey, a great man who became a good friend, was a strong Catholic. He supported the Church and Catholic charities throughout the Boston area. And as I learned quickly, Boston, with its backbone of Irish and Italians, was one of the most Catholic cities in America.)

The next day it was back to haggling with the Sox. Dad, eager to get the deal done for once, came down from his $125,000 demand. The Sox were now offering $108,000, a two-year minor league contract and the rest of my college tuition. I looked at Dad. He didn't come up with any new demands. Me, I was feeling there was something preordained about playing with the Sox. Right field was still big, but they were the one team that seemed to genuinely care about me and my family. It was already feeling like this was where I was supposed to have ended up.

Maybe it wouldn't be so bad. I signed the contract. Because I was only 19, my dad cosigned.

Well, I was on my way. I was playing for the Boston Red Sox.

Even though I had signed a big contract, Dad let me know he was still making the key decisions…

Every week during my freshman year at Notre Dame, he sent me an envelope with a five-dollar bill in it. That was my allowance. As you can imagine, it made my social life a little challenging. Especially because I had begun to get interested in girls after only having eyes for baseball my whole life. The first week of my sophomore year the envelope arrived from Dad. I opened it up to find…$5.

I called him on the phone.

"Cripes, Dad, I just got a $108,000 signing bonus from the Red Sox! I think I deserve a little more than five bucks each week—do you have any idea how hard it is to live on this?"

Another envelope arrived the next week. There was $7.50 in it. **8**

IT'S NOT JUST AN ADVENTURE, IT'S A JOB

Life in the Minors

$93°$ in the shade. Humidity off the charts. A few kids and retirees dotted the stands in Fleming Stadium in Wilson, North Carolina, as I walked from the on-deck circle in the top of the ninth. While I toed into the plate and tugged my sweaty jersey away from my body, the pitcher stared in at me. Bob Veale was an intimidating, intense guy who threw pure fire. Sort of a left-handed Bob Gibson. I'd have said Veale threw even harder than Gibson—but most of the pitching I faced then looked to me like it was fired from a bazooka.

I'd been in the Class B Carolina League for two or three weeks and was starting to think I didn't have what it took. So far I'd been a bigger bust than Paul Pettit. I was batting all of .240, and I wasn't hitting home runs. The balls seemed smaller, the bats seemed heavier and second base, where they had me playing, felt like Mars. Just that afternoon I made two errors.

I represented the tying run and last hope for the Raleigh Capitals. We were getting shut out, 2-0, but Veale had walked a few, and there was a guy on first right now. There were also two outs, though, and so far I was 0 for three.

I took a couple of easy strokes and tightened my grip around the bat. *FAWOOM.* A 98-m.p.h. screamer caught me looking. He just got the outside corner. Or so the ump said.

I started talking to myself.

"Stay cool, don't swing too hard, don't go too deep into your crouch..."

WHIFF! I took a killer cut and came up with nothing. Veale's fastball was really jumping.

I straightened myself out, moved off the bag for a moment, adjusted my helmet and stepped back in.

"Be quick, get on top of it, get out in front," I muttered. "Here it comes, be ready now, OK...*unnnh!*"

A curveball. Young hitters stumble over them because they don't see too many in Little League or high school. It's a pitch for grown-up arms, and this one dove down in front of me like it had fallen through a manhole. I was left swinging at the humid air. I heard a smack in the catcher's glove. The game was over.

The other Capitals and I picked up our stuff from the dugout and filed onto the bus to take the long trip back to Raleigh. The air was stifling. I found a seat, way in the back, slouched down into it and pulled my cap down on my head. Maybe I could at least get a quick nap. But I knew all I was going to do was run that last AB over and over in my head.

Gotta be ready for the curve, I'm not hitting those, my position doesn't feel right...

As the bus jounced out of Wilson, I didn't feel like I was going anywhere.

In a lot of ways, the minors were an even bigger transition than college. The hardest part of it was what I had looked forward to most, in fact: playing baseball as a career, day in and day out. Before I was playing a game once or twice a week—but this was work, and you had to show up for it every day whether you felt like it or not.

The whole lifestyle took some getting used to, as well, especially coming from the early-to-bed, early-to-rise routine of farm life and then Notre Dame. The Carolina League had teams in cities all over North Carolina. Whether they were close or far we'd get to them all the same way: by bus. I had never really traveled by bus before, but now I was spending my whole life on one, bumping along, grinding gears. With a late game and a long drive you'd get in at midnight, 2 a.m., sometimes later than that. You'd sleep late, eat whenever you could.

With a bunch of young men living this kind of life, most of them away from home for the first time, there was some letting off steam. That was something I'd never gotten to do at Notre Dame. Four of us lived in a rooming house in Raleigh. When we didn't have to be riding a bus somewhere at night, we'd get one of the older guys to buy some beer for

MY RALEIGH CAPITALS MUG SHOT, LOOKING A BIT CONFUSED

us and we'd have a few. Sometimes a lot more than a few. We'd sing and laugh and make so much guy noise that we didn't hear the landlady knocking on the wall.

The day after one of those nights, I was hanging around the apartment when the door banged open.

"Dad!"

I was completely shocked to see him standing there. But I looked at his face and pulled myself together real quick. It was the same face he had showed to Ray Garland before he kicked him out of the house.

He was steamed.

He walked into the room, grabbed my shirt and shook me, yelling right in my face like a drill sergeant.

"Goddammit, Carl! How many years did we spend trying to get you here?! Are you going to just piss away your career acting like some punk?!! Now cut this crap out!!

"Straighten up or that's it—you're coming home!!"

Then he turned around and left.

I stood there, still shaking. When I calmed down a little, I figured out what had happened. The landlady had complained to the Capitals manager, Ken Deal. Ken knew I was a special case, a "bonus baby" that Mr. Yawkey was expecting big things from. He also knew I was a guy whose dad was very involved in his career. Rather than just talking to me, Deal called Dad. Dad did the Dad thing: he jumped in his car and drove straight down to North Carolina to shake some sense into me. Then he drove right back to Long Island.

Well, I sure didn't want to go through that again. And Dad was right. My focus wasn't there. The discipline, the intensity. This was a new life for me, OK, but I still needed to approach it my way.

I threw myself into extra infield practice, working out at both second and short. I took as much BP as I could, especially after games where I hadn't produced or didn't feel my swing was right.

One day around that time, when I was still struggling at the plate, Ken Deal drew me aside and offered to work with me. He pointed out that I was standing in the middle of the batter's box so that I had to lunge out in front to connect. That was taking me off balance and making me an easy out.

So I tried moving myself up in the box and—*Crack*—I hit the skin off the ball, sending it over the wall. And I continued hitting the skin off it. I was connecting. My power and average shot up. I hit .400 the rest of the season, felt loose and natural doing it and helped the Capitals turn their fortunes around. I busted out with a two-home-run game and went on a tear that propelled us to a fifteen-game winning streak. While we didn't win the championship in the end, I did get the Carolina league batting crown with a .377 average. I was also Carolina Rookie of the Year and Player of the Year.

As our season was winding down in September, Deal called me in to his office and told me I was going to Minneapolis to help them in the American Association play-offs. The Minneapolis Millers were a Triple A club, the Sox's top farm team.

I was getting kicked up to the next rung of the ladder.

But Deal told me I was going to be taking a detour while my Triple A eligibility got sorted out.

"The Red Sox want you to stop in Boston so they can look you over."

As I walked up to the park I was overcome by a case of the jitters. I hadn't been to Fenway in nearly a year, since I signed before Thanksgiving. At the time, the whole experience was kind of unreal. Now, because I was actually in the organization, seeing the difference between a major league ballpark and a minor league one brought it all home. Fenway looked so big, so important. This was what it was all about—the top of the heap, the big leagues, the Show. These guys didn't have to go to Yankee games in a bus.

Would they ask me to stay? Could this be my big break?

The equipment manager, Don Fitzpatrick, took one look at my beat-up spikes and the sweatshirt and came back with a complete uniform, two pairs of new spikes, some bats of my own and enough Red Sox caps for me, my dad and my brother.

"And here," said Fitzie. "Take some balls. There's a dozen here. All autographed, too. Give 'em to your friends."

That helped me settle down. I began to feel like maybe I belonged here—or would soon. But I didn't really feel completely comfortable until I got down on the field, no longer covered in snow, and walked into the batting cage. It's a funny thing. The cage is a place that makes a lot of people kind of nervous, even good hitters. For me, it's the one place

Fenway Park, Where Time Stands Still.

that I'm at home. It's where I'm supposed to be. I look out at the pitcher and the rest of the world just slips away.

A fat one came over the plate. I jumped on it and hit it into the bleachers in right center. I hit a few more into the bullpen. I stepped back from the bag and a slow smile spread across my face.

This was the park I'd told my dad I wasn't going to be able to hit in. The right field I'd never reach. Guess he was right and I was wrong.

Maybe I'd have an OK career with the Red Sox after all.

Then they had me go work out in the infield so they could watch how I was progressing at second base. That felt great, too.

I was still buzzing from the great workout when I got back to the clubhouse and a big guy with a booming voice walked up to me. He stuck his hand out.

"I'm Ted Williams," he said. Like he had to tell me.

"I'm Carl Yastrzemski."

"Yeah, kid, I know all about ya. Now listen—don't let them screw around with your swing. Ever. You understand me?"

I stammered something—promised I wouldn't, I guess—and he walked over to his locker and didn't say anything more to me for the three days I was in Boston.

Later, I met Tom Yawkey in person. As the owner of the Red Sox, he was kind of a legend in baseball, too. I felt comfortable around him right away, though. He smiled, looked me up and down with his friendly blue eyes and stuck out his hand.

"Pleasure to meet you, Carl! You looked just great out there. I was watching you. You're going to be back up here with us real soon."

That made me feel like a million bucks. Or at least $100,000. But I didn't want to have to wait a year or two. Especially not after getting that kind of thumbs-up from Mr. Yawkey, meeting Ted Williams and conquering Fenway's right field.

The Sox trotted me out to introduce me to the reporters. They had been hearing about me since I signed my contract and got my bonus, and thought the club could use me right now. The Sox had gone into a tailspin that year. They were going to finish nineteen games out of first and had fired their manager, Mike Higgins, halfway through the season.

After I made sure they had the spelling of my name right, which took a while, the reporters wanted to know whether I was going to stay in Boston.

I had never faced reporters before. They were impatient and demanding, like they were the ones who owned the club. I mumbled something about doing whatever was best for the team, how all I wanted to do was contribute wherever they needed me and in the meantime stay focused on my hitting.

Billy Jurges, the new manager, helped me out. The Sox had liked what they'd seen of me, he said, but it wouldn't be smart to throw me out in front of sharp, late-season pitching when all I'd seen so far was Class B stuff.

"We don't want him to get discouraged," said Jurges.

I didn't have much time to reflect on the visit to Boston. I was met at the Minneapolis airport, driven right to the stadium, given a uniform and sent out to shortstop in the middle of the American Association play-off series against Omaha. I got a single in the tenth inning and ended up scoring the winning run. Omaha protested my eligibility, though, so they had to replay the whole game without me. We did end up winning the game the next day, though, as well as the second game of the doubleheader, and then headed to Fort Worth for the American Association championship.

I was finally and officially eligible to play by the second game of the series with Fort Worth, and I made up for lost time. I went three for four, with two RBI and three runs. I had hits in every one of the rest of the games. We won the series and it was on to the Junior World Series, played against the International League champs—the Havana Sugar Kings.

The Cuban revolution had just ended in January, and the U.S. still had relations with Cuba, though things were pretty tense. In July, Frank Verdi of the Rochester Red Wings, a Cardinals affiliate at the time, had gotten shot while coaching at third base during a demonstration outside Gran Stadium in Havana. It wouldn't be long until the U.S. stopped recognizing Cuba and tried to get rid of Castro. And it turned out we were the last professional American baseball team ever to play there. For now, though, the Sugar Kings were still a Cincinnati Reds farm team, and we were all just baseball guys with a series to play.

Our biggest problem, in fact, was that the series opened in Minneapolis. Even for someone from Long Island it was unbelievably cold. And the Cubans? They were freezing their butts off. They managed to win the first game, 5-2, in freezing rain. But we took the second game in 30° weather. I think the Cubans were just trying to survive at that point.

BATTING PRACTICE WAS MY COMFORT ZONE

We saw them light a fire in a wastebasket in their dugout.

There were about 2,500 people there to watch the first game, and maybe 1,000 for the second. The third game was snowed out. It didn't take a lot of diplomacy for us all to agree to play the rest of the games in Cuba.

After Minneapolis, Havana felt like a sauna the second we walked out of our plane. We drove from the Havana airport to the city hall in a parade. We had an escort and there were bands playing, but it just wasn't the kind of parade you'd see in America. Soldiers were everywhere and traffic cut through the parade, going 90 miles an hour. Hundreds, maybe thousands of people marched in the streets, chanting things in Spanish, carrying signs, waving guns in the air. We kept hearing gunshots.

"Looks like I'm not on the potato farm anymore," I told myself.

At the stadium the foul lines were marked by soldiers. There were about 3,000 troops in the park—in foul territory, behind the plate, in the stands, in the dugouts. There were more submachine guns than bats, one guy wrote. He was right. And the bats were going fast, along with the balls and mitts. The Cubans were stealing them. Batting practice was cancelled.

We sat in the dugout and waited. And waited. We had "guards," kids who couldn't have been older than 14 or 15. They were right in the dugout with us, waving their carbines around like toys. They kept giving us wild-eyed looks.

Finally, we heard a clattering in the sky above us and the crowd erupted.

"FIDEL! FIDEL!" The fans were going crazy. The kids with the guns fired into the air. We all jumped. I might have said a Hail Mary or two.

Fidel's helicopter came into the stadium and set down between the mound and second base. He jumped out, looking like he always looked, with the beard, cigar, revolver and fatigues. The guy certainly had a sense of drama.

"I came here to see our team beat Minneapolis," he said in Spanish over the PA system, "not as premier but as just a baseball fan. I want to see our club win the Junior World Series. After the triumph of the revolution, we should also win the Junior World Series."

MY DAYS AT SECOND BASE WOULD BE SHORT-LIVED

We looked at each other. Did that mean we weren't getting out of here alive unless the Sugar Kings won?

The series was really competitive, even though sometimes it was hard to block
out the atmosphere around it. The Sugar Kings were a mix of Cubans and Americans,
with guys like Mike Cuellar and Cookie Rojas who went on to solid careers in the majors.
I hit .312 and blasted a 450-foot homer in the third game that landed right near Fidel. The
Sugar Kings won that night, though, so with Havana leading the series, Fidel decided it
was safe to pay us a visit.

He was a baseball guy, a pitcher who'd gotten himself a tryout with the Senators
way before the revolution. His interpreter said he wanted to meet me. He came up and
shook my hand warmly. The thing that struck me most about him was that huge beard.

"Grand home run!" he said in English, giving me a big smile. I thanked him. Then
he said something else in Spanish.

The interpreter told me, "He wants to know how a man your size could hit the ball so far."

We forced a seventh game. Fidel made his way around the warning track to get to his box seat. Lefty Locklin, our reliever, said that as he passed our bullpen, he paused, patted his service revolver and said, "Tonight, we win." Later on, after Tom Umphlett ended Havana's half of the inning with a nice catch in center field, a soldier made a slicing motion across his throat at us.

Well, that night they did win, taking the Junior World Series, but they won fair and square in the bottom of the ninth with an RBI single and some hard running at the plate. Fidel shook our hands and said, "If there's anything I can do, give me a call."

Mauch took him up on that. Our "getaway" celebration got way out of hand, with guys throwing glasses in the pool, in the street, at cars. Soldiers showed up on our floor. Things were getting ugly.

Gene Mauch was a great manager, and I thought the Red Sox made a mistake in not making him their skipper. He steered us through the next few hours with more tactical skill and guts than most managers show in a lifetime. Mauch said that he was going to call Castro, and he said it loud enough that the soldiers froze. He grabbed a sergeant and went over to a phone. Sure enough, Fidel showed up in our hallway. He and Mauch huddled for a while, then Mauch tells us we're leaving in 20 minutes. Castro personally escorted us to the airport. There was a lot of searching of luggage and at least one more call to Fidel as we sat around for more than four hours waiting for Mauch to buy our way out of there. Finally, he came in and said, "OK, everybody on the plane! Now! Let's go!"

The cheers when it took off might have been louder than when the Sox won the pennant.

I headed back to Notre Dame, a month late for fall semester. People would ask me,

"Hey, Carl—how was your summer? Did you do anything interesting?"

"Ah," I said, "nothing much. I just worked."

My performance with Minneapolis finally won me playing time with the big league club.

The Red Sox invited me to their 1960 spring training. They'd put my locker right next to Ted Williams's. This was his last season, and maybe my first.

The press ate it up. Every day they wanted to know what wisdom the Splendid Splinter was sharing with his protégé, Yastrzemski. I always said something noncommittal about how much I was learning, but it was enough for some trumped-up article under a picture they'd snapped of us together.

What you didn't see in those shots was that I was actually trying to get away from the guy.

In the first place, I was petrified of him. The guy was huge, 6'2" and nearing 240 late in his career, and he had a booming voice. It was common knowledge that he had a terrible temper and cussed people out right and left. Especially when they weren't able to keep up with him.

He was actually friendly, as it turned out. Well, some of the time. And he wanted to talk to me about baseball. The problem was, I had no idea what he was saying.

Ted Williams was the greatest hitter who ever lived. He was a total natural, a guy who hit .400 and made it look easy. He'd also had 22 years in the major leagues to practice hitting, think about hitting, refine hitting and develop a science of hitting. Heck, the guy wrote a book about it. He had some of the most advanced ideas out there about baseball, and here he was trying to pour all that wisdom into this clueless kid in a couple short weeks. He'd grab me, drill me on the stuff.

"Think about the push swing—you want a 90-degree impact from the direction of the pitch."

"Where do you like to see it? What are your zones?"

"Where do you place your weight, kid?"

"You gotta unlock your hips!"

He could just as well have been speaking Greek.

I'd make like I was listening—I mean I tried to, really, but I was a 20-year-old who'd only faced a few weeks of Triple A pitching. And now here I was going up against the likes of Juan Marichal. It was all I could do to take care of the basics.

The basics were working pretty well, actually. I was batting .360 that spring, blasting homers, knocking in runs. My mom and dad had come down to Scottsdale, Arizona, and I lit up the San Francisco Giants with them in the stands. I homered, drove in four runs and played errorless second base, pivoting on double plays like I'd been doing it forever.

"I'm gonna make the club this year," I said to my dad. "I know it." I was hot...and the Sox were not. They'd had a losing record the year before, finishing fifth in the AL.

Dad wasn't so sure that was their game plan.

"Now, they may have other ideas for you, Carl."

And sure enough, suddenly they stopped playing me. Then they just as suddenly sent me down to the minors again.

I don't know when I'd been so mad.

Here I was with the Sox, they needed me, I was doing great. Fantastic, even. It just didn't make any sense.

Gene Mauch met me at the airport the evening I landed in Deland, Florida, where the Millers trained.

"Feel like a workout?" he asked me when we got in the car.

"What? Now? Jeez, Gene, it's..." I looked at my watch, trying to figure out what time zone I was in. "...uh, dinnertime. What workout are you talking about?"

He looked at me.

"Do you have any idea why you're here, Carl?"

"Not really," I said. I shoved my hands in my pockets, looked at my shoes and felt mad all over again.

"We're switching you to left field."

Left field?? I fell back in the seat. The whole thing suddenly came into focus.

Left field was Ted Williams's position!

That changed everything. It was probably their plan from day one. Now that Williams was retiring, it was time to start training me to play in left against the Green Monster. Wow. I was proud, I was excited, I was kind of nervous.

A whole new jumble of thoughts started to bump the anger and frustration out of their way.

Mauch was right. I needed to start learning the outfield. No time to lose. For one thing, I'd never played much of it except for a little time in center field with the White

Eagles. And playing with those teams meant fields without fences—running and running until you tripped over a rock, and got too tired to hit. In pro baseball there would be none of that. It was just a matter of knowing the dimensions of the park you were playing in. And that was particularly true of left field in Fenway.

There was another thing, too, something I think Mauch got. I've got to be working at something or I go crazy. Like my pitching back when I was a kid. Working with my batting gadgets, becoming a slugger. Learning second base well enough to go from 45 errors in Class B to eventually feeling I could challenge the Red Sox's Pete Runnels for a job. My focus and intensity are so strong they begin to eat away at me unless I'm working on my game. Mauch could probably see I was burned up by being sent down, and he wasted no time in helping me channel that energy.

Mauch and Chuck Tanner, another coach, worked with me over the next few weeks, hitting me fungoes. First I was just shagging flies. Easy stuff, getting used to the arc of the ball out there. Then I worked on grounders, which come at you differently in the outfield. Mauch and Tanner were letting me figure most of this stuff out myself, like the unconventional way I went at grounders using only my glove hand.

I've always thought I was lucky to learn the outfield so late in my career; no one showed me how to do it.

Next thing I knew, Mauch was gone. He'd been hired by Philadelphia. Their gain, our loss. He was a smart guy and a great manager. Eddie Popowski, Gene Mauch's replacement at Minneapolis, had been in the Sox's farm system forever, working with younger guys at the Class D and Double A levels. He would prepare me to play the Wall.

Fenway fans know that big thing in left field as the Green Monster. To players who live next to it half the year, staring up at all the different surfaces and features that can make a ball bounce off it a hundred different ways, it's the Wall. It's a piece of real estate you won't find the likes of which anywhere in baseball. And it gives the Red Sox a big home field advantage—if their left fielder knows how to play it.

Nicollet Park in Minneapolis didn't have a high wall anything like the Wall. Nor did most of the other stadiums we played in in the American Association. Houston and Fort Worth did, though. Whenever the Millers were in Texas, Pop ran outfield workouts at the park before a night game. He was hitting fungoes to me by 10 a.m.

He'd have me turn my back to him as soon as he hit it. The point was to get the

TED WILLIAMS TELLING IT LIKE IT IS TO A SCRAWNY ROOKIE (ME)

rebound off the wall, then wheel around and throw it. I'd spent the whole last season learning how to pivot on the double play, but this was something completely new. Now, I'd always had a cannon for an arm. So the distance to the infield wasn't much of a problem. Because the ball takes longer to get there, though, you need to learn to think in a new way about which base to throw to, and you have to understand who your cutoff men are.

It was a lot to chew on. And even though I'd hit well at the end of the last season and in spring training, I was still getting used to Triple A pitching. I started to struggle at the plate. Popowski and the other coaches didn't seem to be able to help me with my hitting. So I called my dad. Mom and Dad drove straight to Nicollet Park from Long Island, driving in shifts, and arrived there the next day. Dad was all business. He got out of the car, nodded at me, shook hands with Popowski and stood there while Pop threw me BP.

After a while Dad waved Popowski off, came up to the cage and said, "You're crouching too much, Carl. Straighten up. And here," he said, adjusting my bat angle, "now try that."

Dad stepped back from the cage and nodded for the pitch like he was the manager. Popowski raised his eyebrow, threw one down the middle and—*Crack*—I smashed into the ball. It sailed into the seats in center right. *Crack*. Another one. *Crack*. Another.

Mom and Dad stayed to see our game that evening. I got three hits. As they drove back to Long Island the next day, Popowski told me, "Next time you need him, don't hesitate. Just pick up that phone and give him a ring!"

I kept on hitting as the season went on, and started to hit better and better. From August through the end of the season I was hitting at an insane pace, almost .500. Factoring in my slump at the start of the year I finished at .339, which didn't win me the batting title. But it was good enough for American Association MVP. The difference was my outfield play. I had a .981 fielding percentage and 18 assists in left. My game was coming together.

I was ready for the majors.

I bought a house in Lynnfield, Massachusetts, and decided that was the end of shuttling around the country for my education. I finally finished my business degree in 1966 at nearby Merrimack College—with a lot of help from the profs there, and flexibility from the Augustinian fathers who ran the place. When a pennant went up in front of the school saying YAZ WENT TO SCHOOL HERE when we won the pennant in '67, some of them wanted to add: THE HELL HE DID. **8**

Red Sox
TEAM
||
Carl Yastrzemski
PLAYER
|

||0 3| 65
CHAPTER NO.

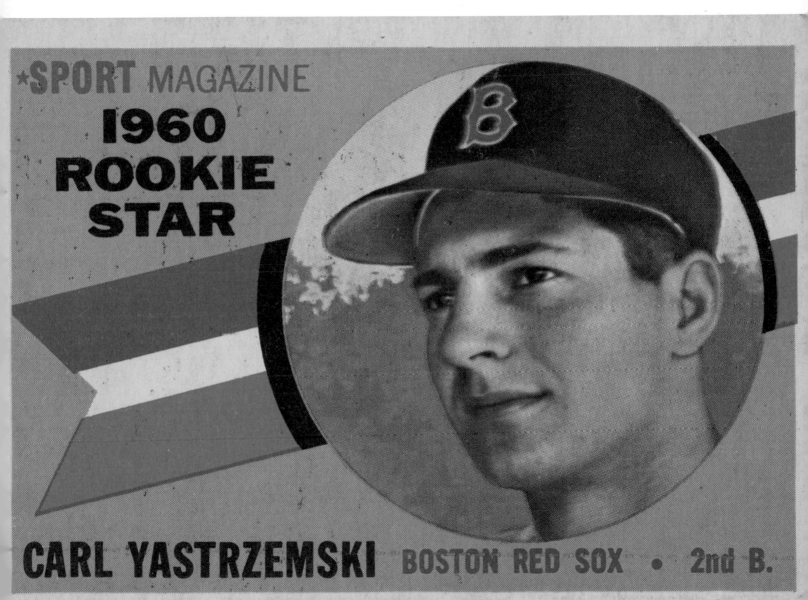

YASTRZEMSKI BASEBALL CARD 1960

WELCOME TO THE SHOW

Y as vs. Ted. I choked on my cornflakes.

I was reading through the *Boston Globe* while I ate breakfast on April 12, 1961. We'd opened against the Kansas City Athletics the day before. There, in the sports section, was a new little box that showed how I did in my first Opening Day compared to how Ted Williams had done in his (I got a single, he got a double). The comparison box was going to be a regular feature. Every game. Me...versus Ted.

Wonderful. Just what I needed.

I understood it, sure; there had been some lackluster years in Boston. The sportswriters were looking for something to get excited about. They had made a big deal over me when I came to visit Boston in late '59. Then they'd started to play up the Yaz-Ted connection in the last year's spring training. Now, finally, here I was in the Red Sox lineup. Boston's next great hope.

I had gotten my first major league hit on Opening Day, a single to left center off Ray Herbert. I remember breathing a sigh of relief when I reached first—good to get that out of the way, I thought. But then our manager, Mike Higgins, gave me the steal sign. Maybe to give me some practice at stealing, maybe to keep me from making too much of the hit and losing my focus. Whatever, the A's catcher, Haywood Sullivan (who would

"He reminded me of myself. He's wound up like a clock. He's ready to go." -*Ted Williams about me*

later become the Sox's GM and then the co-owner of the team), threw me out at second. It really wasn't all that close. After that I struck out twice, grounded out and flied out. I certainly hadn't set the world on fire.

Apparently, though, I didn't play badly enough to snuff out the hype—or the expectations.

The box kept running and the articles and columns kept coming as the season went on, but there was more and more disappointment in them. There were also more catcalls from the critics in the left field seats. There was no way around it: I was struggling. My average hovered around .210.

I'd won a batting title and an MVP in the minors, but it might as well have been a merit badge in the Cub Scouts. The pitching I'd seen there had nothing to do with the stuff they threw in the majors. The fastballs were jumpier, the curveballs dropped harder and the pitchers were smarter.

Nobody was saying it, but I was sure people in the Red Sox management were thinking, "The kid's just not ready yet." I was starting to get benched for right-handers, or just "rested" for a few days.

There was so much to adjust to: the dimensions of all the different AL parks, the Wall in Fenway, the blinding afternoon sun in Yankee Stadium, how slow Whitey Ford's curveball was. To be "the next Ted Williams" on top of all that was killing me.

I had worked with Williams that last spring training. When he wanted to show me something he'd take the bat out of my hands and stand in himself. I couldn't believe how effortlessly he swatted the ball out of the park, how quick his wrists were, even at age 43. I knew that as good as I got—if I got to be good at all—I'd never be anything like him.

"There was a very long tradition of Fenway Park excellence to live up to."

I would have liked to come in unnoticed. But there was no way that was going to happen. And the constant media attention built up the expectations of the fans when I took over left field. All that pressure was the toughest thing I had to face; it almost cost me my ability to make the big leagues.

(TOP) BABE RUTH, ERNIE SHORE, RUBE (GEORGE) FOSTER AND DEL GAINER AT THE EDGE OF THE RED SOX DUGOUT AT FENWAY PARK (1915). THEY BEAT THE PHILADELPHIA PHILLIES 4 GAMES TO 1 TO WIN THE WORLD SERIES. (BOTTOM) BOBBY DOERR, DOM DIMAGGIO, JOHNNY PESKY, RUDY YORK AND TED WILLIAMS HIT THE RED SOX INTO THE 1946 WORLD SERIES. THEY WERE EDGED OUT BY THE ST. LOUIS CARDINALS 4 GAMES TO 3.

Here was the biggest critic of all, though: me. I've always had to be the best. If I'm going to do something, I'm going to kill myself until I can do it at the highest level. I'm rarely satisfied, either. I always think I need to do better.

Take 1960, when I won the American Association MVP. Sure, it was nice to have it, but the truth was that I was really mad at losing the batting title by .003 points. When I finally got up to the major leagues I felt like I should have an immediate impact, without needing any adjustment to the speed and power of the major league game, and that I should be hitting with a high average and a lot of home runs. The fans expected it, I told myself. So I was trying to knock every single pitch out of the park.

I was trying way too hard. I was getting in my own way.

My problems weren't all psychological, though. There were technical bugs. Things I didn't understand. I was still so green I didn't even know enough to know what questions to ask.

Opposing pitchers weren't helping. They know how to mess with rookies. Once someone saw he could jam me pretty easily inside, it seemed like every pitcher in the AL was jamming me inside. It's a tight fraternity, pitching. Word gets around. These guys were relentless.

June 14, Detroit. Frank Lary had just jammed me on a 1-1 fastball my first time up at Tiger Stadium that day, shattering the bat.

Now that's a bad feeling. When the ball comes in on you tight and hits the "Hiller-ich & Bradsby" trademark of your Louisville Slugger, it makes a kind of sickening snapping noise, nothing at all like the *Crack* when you get a really solid hit from the sweet spot. The bat splinters instantly and you're just swinging a sawed-off stump. There's nothing there at the other end. You feel like you're going to fall over.

The ball dribbled weakly to second, and I was out by a mile.

This kind of thing is worse when you're having an 0-for-four day. It's worse still when your batting average is tumbling towards .200.

I guess I was lucky just to get jammed; Lary hit nineteen batters in 1961, almost

"NO ONE PLAYED THE GAME LIKE TED WILLIAMS."

a record. That didn't matter to me then, though. I was just trying to figure him out. Hey, I was trying to figure out major league pitching in general. Okay, what was it Williams had taught me in the spring? Look for the pitch he got you with last time.

Well, he got me with a slider in my first at bat. I'll look for that my second time up. Right. I was still looking for it when the third sinker whizzed right by me. So next time I expected the sinker and he struck me out with sliders, jamming me like my first time up. The fourth time he mixed it up, almost splitting my bat again. I was out easily on a weak roller.

Fitzie, our equipment guy, came over to console me on the flight back to Boston. I was grousing about my situation, feeling sorry for myself. Then, talking to Fitzie, I got the idea to speak to Mr. Yawkey about it. After all, part of the pressure I was feeling was that he wasn't getting much of a return from all this money he'd invested in me.

Fitzie said that'd be a great idea.

I liked Mr. Yawkey and I could see he liked me. I didn't know him very well then, but somehow I felt comfortable around him. There was just something very real and direct about Mr. Yawkey. I met him in his Fenway office and told him I felt like I was letting him down. For him, it was a nonissue. He smiled at me the way your favorite uncle would, and patted me on the back.

"Carl, you're young, still getting used to the big leagues! You'll come around. I don't have any doubt about that. You're a natural!"

It was nice that Mr. Yawkey was behind me. Especially as he was writing my checks. But it wasn't enough. I was jumping out of my skin. It was killing me, not hitting. I needed help, and I needed it now.

"Well, thanks, Mr. Yawkey, but it's...it's eating me up inside. I'm really stuck. I just have to be able to do better than this! I wish Ted were here."

Mr. Tom Yawkey was a dear friend who cared deeply about his players.

He asked Ted Williams to come back to groom his new left fielder.

When preparation meets opportunity, good things can happen.

Since retiring, Williams was a special batting instructor for the Sox. He'd spent a lot of time with me during spring training in 1961, and it had helped a lot. His pointers couldn't have been more different than the high-flown baseball theory he was throwing at me in 1959. He'd explain them, demonstrate them and drill me on them whenever I saw him—in the locker room, the parking lot, anywhere.

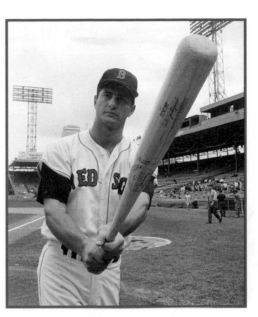

"Let's go through this again," he'd say. "Four things, kid. What's the first one?"

"Close your stance and back away."

"What's the second?"

"Watch the ball."

"Right. The third?"

"Hit the ball through the middle."

"The fourth thing? What's the fourth thing?"

"Be quick."

"Yes! Be quick, dammit, be quick."

As I went through the lineup of American league pitchers this season, it felt like Williams's principles of hitting were the only thing keeping me in the game. I'd mumble them to myself when I stood at the plate. In one way, his rules were real direct and common-sense. But there was so much of Ted's thinking and experience behind each one that they always worked a lot better when he was walking me though them himself.

Mr. Yawkey brightened up and leaned against his desk.

"You want Ted? Yes, yes...that could be the answer. Let's get Ted up here!" He turned around, grabbed the phone and put a call through right away. Turned out Williams was in a boat miles off the New Brunswick coast, going after some fish or other. Now that he'd retired from baseball he was one of the best anglers in the world. He'd written a book on that, too.

But when Mr. Yawkey called, people answered—wherever they were. The next morning, Williams was leaning against the rail at Fenway, waiting for me.

"Hello, Yaz!" he roared at me. His voice was so huge I felt like I had to hang on to something when he greeted me. "How are you? Now what the hell's the matter?"

We talked for a while in the dugout. Williams was friendly and helpful. He told me not to be afraid to ask him anything. Except for his booming voice, he seemed like a completely different person than the impatient, intimidating giant he was when I'd first met him. We went over everything I had been doing. Then we went over to the cage and Williams watched me hit.

After a couple of pitches he asked me, "What's going on with that crouch?"

"Crouch?"

"Yeah, you're in a crouch!" It was so slight that nobody had noticed, especially not me. But Ted Williams was Ted Williams, who understood batting like few other people have ever been able to. To him, the contrast between my stance now and what it had been like in spring training was enormous.

"Straighten up a little, Yaz! That's right, now you can use your knees more to move within your stance."

I did as he said and after a few more pitches was hitting the ball a lot more solidly.

The pitcher, Joe Coleman, was a former major leaguer who'd been with the old Philadelphia A's for many years.

"OK, Joe, now jam him!"

I moved deeper in the box, like Williams had showed me.

"That's it, Yaz!" he said. "Just take your natural swing. Hit down the middle. That's right…"

At another point he stopped Coleman and said, "Dammit, Yaz, look at you. Look at how much of your body you're using. The whole thing, really—it's in the hands, the hands." Easy for him to say. He was Ted Williams.

He picked up a bat and had Coleman pitch to him. Even then, retired and middle-aged, his wrists were phenomenally quick. As much as I developed through my career, getting over 400 home runs and more than 3,000 hits, I never had wrists like that. He was parking them all over the right field bleachers with these effortless flicks.

I got back in, tried to mimic him and knocked a few into the seats.

"Good, Yaz! Good!"

The lesson went on a little while longer. When he was sure I felt comfortable and remembered everything he'd told me, he waved goodbye, walked through a tunnel and headed back to Canada, where he got on his fishing boat and headed out into the Atlantic again.

I couldn't wait for the game to start that night. The stuff Ted had told me in spring, well, there was always something just a little mysterious about it. I knew there was more to those "four things" than he was telling me. But this time, I really felt like I got it. There was only one way to find out.

I hit two doubles that night, and I kept going from there, batting .478 through July. 22 hits in 46 at bats. I closed out the season with a .266 average. Not great, by any means, but considering where I'd been at the beginning of the season, I'd live with it. I was seeing the pitchers again as we played ball clubs a second or third time in the season. I was learning their stuff. I was also adjusting to big league fastballs. Curveballs weren't fooling me as badly, either. For the first time in a while I could see light at the end of the tunnel.

I was actually looking forward to the next season to show the Red Sox they hadn't made a mistake signing Carl Yastrzemski.

But there was the defensive side of my game to figure out, too.

"The Wall, kid," Eddie Popowski would say when he was teaching me fielding. He'd shake his head and look into the distance like he was seeing something that I could never imagine.

"Nothing we do is going to prepare you for it—not really."

He was right.

I'd only been at Fenway twice, and my main concern then had been right field: was I going to be able to hit it out? April 11, 1961, was my first time on the grass as left fielder.

I walked over to left. The nearer I got to the Wall, the smaller I felt.

The Wall is 37 feet, 2 inches high. It's the highest wall in baseball. And it's green. No wonder fans call it the Green Monster. Red Sox players tend to call it the Wall, though, because of their point of view: looking up at it from the bottom, trying to hit balls over it. Another thing, I think, is that when you call it the Wall, that tells you it's an obstacle. A big challenge for left fielders and line-drive home run hitters. A lot of guys who hit tape-measure home runs in other parks just got "Wall-ball doubles" off it.

But there's so much more to it than its height if you're playing left field. Try to follow me here and you'll get a sense of how hard it was to field a ball off it.

The first 25 feet of the Wall are concrete. After that it's wood, which when I was the regular left fielder was covered in tin. (They covered it with some kind of Formica plastic stuff in '76.) So if it's not going to clear the Wall, you have to make your first decision: is it going to hit the cement (big rebound) or the tin (dead drop)? The tin was attached to the

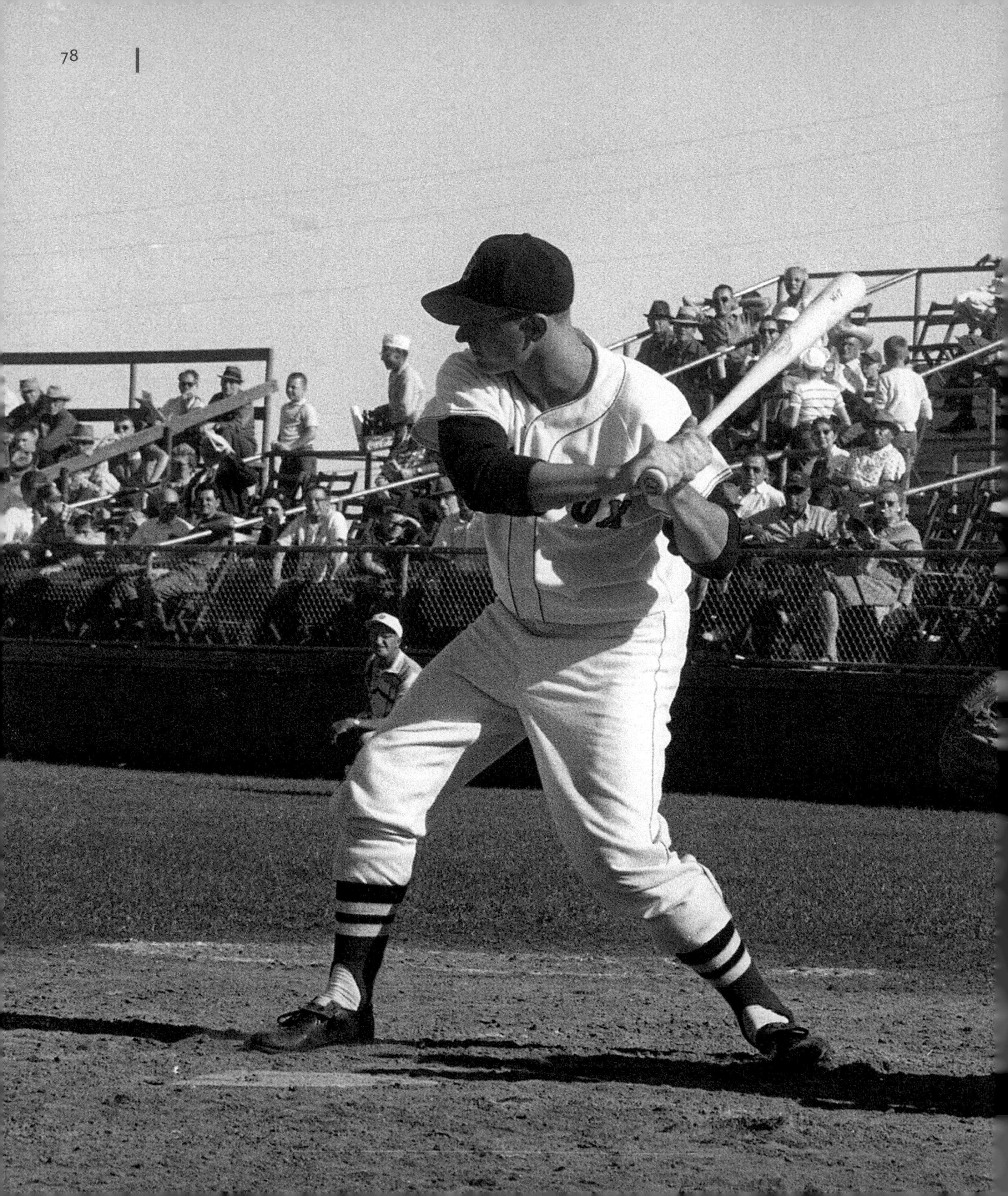

wood and steel girders behind it with exposed rivets—so next you have to ask yourself, is it going to hit the rivets? If it did, it would ricochet in some crazy direction, right or left. Which way it would go would depend a lot on the rotation of the ball, and that's different for right-handed batters and lefties like me. And there were gaps in the tin in some places, where the wood or even a steel girder was exposed, which sent the ball bounding back into the field when you were expecting a straight drop from the tin.

Wait. There's even more. There's a thirteen-foot-high, old-fashioned scoreboard that sticks out from the bottom of the Wall. It's a manually operated board, now the last one in the majors. The ball can carom off the top of the scoreboard and take a whole new flight path. Also, there are these notches that guys slide the numbers in and out of. Balls can hit those, which tweaks the ricochet.

Oh, I almost forgot the ladder. A ladder goes up from the scoreboard to the top of the Wall for pulling balls out of the netting they used to have there. They took away the netting to put some seats in, but they left the ladder attached to the Wall for future left fielders to worry about. I never had a ball hit into it when I was fielding. You had to look out for it, though. In 1963, we had a slugger named Dick Stuart—a big, lumbering guy who couldn't outrun a glacier. He hit an inside-the-park home run off that ladder. The ball bounced into the left field corner, where it's hard to corral a ball if you don't know the park. By the time the Indians' left fielder ran the ball down, Stuart had managed to get himself around the bases.

That corner actually sits behind the end of the third base side stands, which jut out into left. There's a doorway where the ball can get stuck, too. The visitors' dugout is on the third base line, so their view of the corner is blocked by the stands. Their left fielders would seem to disappear sometimes. Don Baylor of the Orioles had his teammates worried when he chased a carom into the corner and was trying to pull the ball out of the doorway; to the Orioles, he'd just vanished, with our guys circling the bases. They all stuck their heads out of the dugout. Earl Weaver, their manager, thought we'd kidnapped Baylor, or that maybe we had a trapdoor out there, too.

Those stands only leave three precious feet of foul territory. First you had to learn how not to smash your knees running right into them, and then how you could use them to push off and make great throws into second base.

You had a very cozy relationship with the fans when you played left field in

Boston. Fenway fans are harsh judges. They'd judged Ted Williams and they judged me. And they aren't afraid to let you know their opinions. In general, though, they were my greatest supporters. They cheered me on for every fielding move I made and congratulated me after a good turn at the bat in the bottom of the last inning.

"Great hit, Yaz!"

"Way to go, Yaz!"

"Hell of a catch, Yaz!"

"Ya got it, Yaz—*yaaaa gooooooooot iiiiiit!*"

They were my competitors, too—a long foul meant I'd be fighting for the ball with lots of hands, mitts and caps shoved out into that tiny foul territory.

My first game nobody was too impressed with my batting, but I won a lot of the left field crowd over with my glove. In the second inning, the A's Leo Posada was on second with Sullivan, the catcher, at the plate. Sullivan hit a hot grounder that got by Pete Runnels, who was playing third. Going on pure instinct—and adrenaline—I charged in and snagged the ball with the one-handed scoop I'd been practicing in the minors. I threw home on the run as Posada rounded third. The throw beat him by a mile—Russ Nixon tagged him out and the crowd went wild—it felt like there was an earthquake out there in left. I'd just won myself a lot of fans.

But when I was looking up at the Wall that first time, I knew I was looking at the biggest challenge an outfielder could face. I swallowed. My palms got a little sweaty. I'm a competitive guy, though. Throw an obstacle at me and that becomes my goal: overcoming it and being that much better. I was determined to play Fenway's left field better than anyone ever had or ever would.

The thing is, Pop was right. There was nothing like the Wall anywhere, and there was no instruction manual. The guy who'd been here for 22 years, Ted Williams, never said anything about it. And besides, I needed to focus on hitting every second I was with him. So I really just had to teach myself how to play left field when I finally got to Fenway.

Or maybe I should say I had to let the Wall teach me. I learned by trial and error how the ball bounced off each part of it, and how hard, and in what direction. I learned to tell from the arc of the ball what part of the Wall it was going to hit. I got to know all the holes in the scoreboard, where the rivets were and all the other little nooks and crannies that made life so interesting out there.

OAK 0 0 0

BOSTON 2 0 0

BAT — BALL —

Left field at Fenway is short. 310 feet? 315 feet? 304.7 feet? It depends who you ask. The Red Sox won't let you measure it. Whatever it is, it's short. And that meant that there were a lot of home runs hit out onto Lansdowne. If you could get enough height on the ball. Sometimes people said that made the Red Sox a team of lazy, right-handed hitters.

Yeah, right. I was neither.

It's not like we were the only team hitting over the Wall, though. The name Bucky Dent gives a lot of Sox fans fits. They know him by names I can't use in this book. He made the Wall even more (in)famous by skying one over it in our one-game play-off with the Yankees in 1978. I wasn't playing left field much anymore at that point in my career, but I was that day. And there was nothing I could do.

But because left is short and the Wall is high, you gave up as many homers as you hit. It turned them into Wall-ball doubles instead. And if you were a fielder who knew how to play the Wall, you could turn those doubles into singles, and take away runs, too.

I learned to use the Wall to decoy batters. My "dekes," I called them. I'd make them think it was a routine fly ball, just kind of staring up at it, maybe bringing my glove up. So the runner would just slowly trot to first, assuming I'd catch it. But then it would go off the Wall, like I knew it would, and I'd whirl around, grab it and hold him to a single. Maybe there'd be a runner on second and he'd hold up. By the time it hit the Wall, he could only advance to third.

I liked to make a guy think his long fly ball was a homer. I'd hang my head, kick the ground. The goal was to slow him down on the bases; nobody runs the bases at full speed when he doesn't have to. He'd go into his home run trot, real easy, and suddenly, just at the last second, I'd whip around, grab the ball off the Wall, fire it to second—and maybe even get him out.

There are no records on it, but I know my dekes saved us a lot of runs. Sometimes I think I should have gotten an Oscar.

When enough guys got fooled with this I realized I couldn't run my dekes all the time, so I had to start saving them for late innings where the game was on the line. Then again, once teams had seen me, they figured out that with my arm, in that park, they weren't going to have much success running on me. They'd gamble only when it counted. So I had 'em psyched out without even having to run the dekes.

One deke didn't have any practical purpose—it was more psychological. Or just for pride. If one of their guys hit one that was obviously headed for the street, I'd just stand there looking forward towards the infield. Wouldn't even acknowledge the thing.

It used to drive our pitchers crazy. Bill Monbouquette would say, "Aw, come on, Yaz, can't you at least make it look like you can catch it?" But I knew when the ball was going out. I just didn't want to give the hitter the satisfaction of turning around.

Also, I admit, it could be kind of a comment when I did that—a message to our pitcher. Like maybe his pitch selection could have been a little better.

I didn't master the Wall in my first game, or in my first year or two. My second year, 1962, I led the league in assists—but also in errors by an outfielder. Some of those eleven errors were "Wall errors." You tended to learn how to play it through your mistakes. But a lot of my errors were throwing errors. I had that cannon arm, and I wasn't afraid to use it. Being young, aggressive and inexperienced, though, sometimes I'd throw wildly, or bypass the cutoff man when I shouldn't have, or just misjudge how fast guys could run in the majors. As late as 1963 I was still making those mistakes—I lost a game by overthrowing the catcher that year, which let the winning run score. The guys said, "Nice parachute throw!" when I came into the clubhouse after it was over, and laughed at me. That burned me up.

Over the years, though, I got to know that Wall—and my arm—pretty well. As the years went on, I got fewer and fewer assists at Fenway; it got to where nobody would run on me.

Some baseball "experts" say I got more credit for being a great outfielder than I deserved because Fenway's left is so short. Sure it's short. But that just makes the Wall that much more of a factor. I'd like to see those guys play it. It's not as easy as it looks.

As soon as the last game of the '61 season was over, I was on my way back to school. I was pretty relieved to have my first season in the big leagues behind me. Considering that I stunk the place up when I showed up, my .266 finish wasn't bad at all. I'd hit about .300 since Ted Williams had showed me the light, led the team in doubles and total bases and was second in RBI, with 80. I was pretty pleased with what I'd accomplished and began to think that Mr. Yawkey might be right. I sure wasn't going to say I was a natural, but just maybe I was coming around.

In 1961, I'd been more focused on how I was doing as a baseball player than how we were doing as a team. I had to be. But a complete ballplayer helps his team. The Red Sox finished in sixth place in 1961. In '62, I wanted to start winning ball games. I wanted to chase after a pennant.

Well, it was a nice thought, anyway. 8

THE DOLDRUMS

"Yastrzemski...I tell ya. Kid's not pulling his weight."

Waste of money, you ask me. Yawkey makes him the richest kid in town when we coulda spent it getting some decent pitching or..."

"Or paying us what we're worth!"

"Yeah!"

Then, laughter.

Sure, guys, yuk it up.

Maybe they didn't know I was the one in the shower. Maybe they thought I'd already left.

Maybe they wanted me to hear.

It was June 1962. We'd just been bombed by the Kansas City A's 9-2, our third loss in a row. After going hitless in four at bats, I took batting practice after the game. So yes, I was still there, and I could hear every word.

The Sox were in ninth place nine and a half games out, and we weren't going to get much closer. We'd finish the season nineteen games behind the Yankees. With Ted Williams gone and us becoming a second-division team, fewer and fewer fans were coming to the park.

There's always tension on a losing team. Bad tension. Guys had to take it out on someone. They saw this kid who hadn't done much but take a lot of cash they figured should be going to them, with the club having an even worse finish than the previous year.

The whispers started in spring training. Mutters, looks— the silent treatment. I had become the whipping boy for the Red Sox—me and my $108,000 bonus.

The irony was that I had finished strong the last year and started strong in '62. I wasn't the second coming of Ted Williams—I was barely Carl Yastrzemski yet. But I was showing people that I could hit major league pitching and give the Sox something extra in the outfield. That only seemed to make matters worse, though. It was as if some guys would have preferred me to be a total bust. Maybe that would have confirmed their feeling that no rookie was worth the money I was getting.

It was tough on me. I thought it was going to be different being a big-league baseball player. I'd imagined that my teammates would be pros, not jealous and petty as a bunch of kids—and that they'd be passionate about the game like I was. I remembered how much fun it was back with the White Eagles or my Bridgehampton High team when we won a big game—the whooping and hollering. Or even groaning about a loss together. The shouldas and couldas. There's nothing like being able to share your excitement with 24 or more other guys, the thrill of victory, agony of defeat, the whole ball of wax.

True, there wasn't a lot to holler about, going 75-85. But there wasn't a lot of team chemistry, either. The clubhouse was like a morgue. I'd noticed that right away when I got there in '61. At the time, I thought maybe I was just getting the cold shoulder because I was a rookie. If anything, though, it was worse in '62. Yaz or no Yaz, there was no excitement to the Red Sox, no heart. Guys were just there collecting a paycheck.

At least the grudge they had against me was giving some guys stuff to grumble about to each other.

Charlie Schilling, my buddy from Long Island and our second baseman, had the locker next to mine. I don't know what I would have done without him. We kept each other from going crazy by talking about the game, even when everyone else seemed to be on autopilot. And there was Fitzie, too. He counseled me to shut out the Yaz trashers, tune out the atmosphere and focus on my game.

"Get out there and hit for yourself," he said. "Hit for your family. Forget about the others—they're losers."

Fitzie was right. So I tried to just keep my
head down and work at improving my game.

By August, even though as a team we were
slipping further and further out of contention, I was
hitting my stride, feeling more and more comfortable at the plate. I would probably have finished
the season over .300, with 20 home runs and more
than 100 RBI, but then I started to feel run down.
I got weird aches and pains in my legs and back. I
could barely drag myself out of bed.

The doctor thought it was nerves. He knew me, and how much I obsessed on my
hitting, my performance, where the team was going. Turned out it was something else,
though: jaundice.

Jaundice! That came out of left field (so to speak). But I decided to keep on playing. Even if the team's season was shot, mine wasn't. I was so close to batting .300. I went
into our final day, a doubleheader against the Senators, batting .295. If I went three for
three in just one of the games, I'd reach .300. I got two hits in the first game, clawing my
way to .297. So I started the second game—but came up empty. Higgins could see I was
drooping. He pulled me after two at bats. Finishing at .296 was good enough for the sec-
ond-highest average on the team that year.

Small consolation for finishing in eighth place, though. Between that and the jaundice, I was in a funk. I was...depressed.

I didn't go back to Notre Dame that fall. (I never did go back as a student, in fact.)
I had hit OK that year, and no longer doubted that I could make it at the major league level.
It was the Red Sox I was having doubts about.

And I wasn't the only one asking those questions. After sixth- and eighth-place
finishes, Mr. Yawkey felt he had to make some changes for 1963. First, he kicked Mike Higgins upstairs to GM and put Johnny Pesky in as manager. Then he brought in slugger Dick
Stuart from the Pirates to knock in more runs.

Pesky was a hometown favorite who'd been the shortstop with Ted Williams on
the Sox's last pennant-winner in 1946. He had part of the park named after him already,

JOHNNY PESKY HAD A CERTAIN CHARM

in fact: Pesky's Pole, in right. He was a compact firecracker of a guy, and a baseball man through and through. He was impatient to win. To me, he got what was wrong with the club: the lackadaisical attitude, the lack of drive. By spring training, when I'd gotten over my jaundice and had had a chance to talk with Pesky, I was believing again. The team started out the season like they believed, too. Pesky was everyplace, managing the hell out of the team, lighting a fire under the guys. The fans were coming to the park again. The Sox were winning. We were nipping at the Yankees' heels. June 28 we took the fight to New York and beat them at their place 4-3. I got two hits and scored a run. We were only one and a half games back. The clubhouse was alive again.

I was having a blast at the plate. Mike Higgins had given me a key pointer in the off-season.

"Look at you, Yaz—you're trying to be Stan Musial!"

Because Stan the Man was left-handed, I loved imitating his stance as a kid, coiled like a corkscrew with my bat held so high my hands were at my ears. I guess I'd kept that habit, or slipped into it unconsciously, even in the major leagues—especially because I was trying to make my mark as a slugger, right from the get-go. Higgins showed me how I'd get the ball on the bat a lot quicker if I lowered the bat.

When I did that, it was easier to make contact. I also naturally hit to get on base rather than out of the park. My average shot up and I started to spray the ball around the field. I was on my way to winning my first AL batting title, with a .321 average. There was a lot less Yaz-razzing in the stands, and more important, I was proving myself to my teammates.

The mutters and whispers stopped. It was fun playing baseball again.

Well, all I can say is that there must have been some sort of dark cloud over the Red Sox in my first six seasons. The sun may have been shining on us for those first few months of '63, but as soon as we won that June game against New York, the skies got dark again. Our pitching couldn't keep pace. We dropped the next four at Yankee Stadium, and kept dropping them until we were 28 games out.

Soon everything was spinning out of control. Pesky lost control of the club. He got into spats with players—especially Stuart, who struck out all the time, couldn't field and didn't give a damn. Stuart bragged about how many homers he hit; Pesky told him he lost more games for us than he won. Stuart told Pesky he didn't feel like he had to listen to him because he made twice as much money as Pesky did. It went on like that all the time, like a bad marriage—in the dugout, in the locker room, on the bus. Pesky should have been above that kind of stuff. The next season, he and I stopped speaking to each other after he demoted Charlie Schilling and then said I wasn't hustling.

The positive energy soured. The locker-room buzz vanished. Same old Red Sox.

By late '64 Pesky was gone. The musical managers game moved on.

Fitzie had a point, but my teammates weren't all losers.

Oh, we had our characters, there was no denying that. If characters thrive in baseball, then the Red Sox are a greenhouse for 'em. Later in my career, Red Sox Bill "Spaceman" Lee and Wade Boggs provided all the color the press wanted. When I broke in, pitcher Gene Conley was our comic relief.

A hell of an athlete, Conley stood 6'8" and starred in two sports: during our offseason he played basketball with the Celtics. He was probably the most popular guy on the club because of his size, his smile and his loopiness. Conley had a habit of just vanishing. He'd walk out of the stadium with us, but then when Higgins took a head count on the bus, Conley wasn't there. Sometimes he wouldn't make plane flights, either. You wouldn't see him for days.

For someone close to seven feet tall, he sure was elusive.

Conley's best remembered for the time in '61 when he stood up and got off the bus in the middle of a traffic jam in the Bronx. He took infielder Pumpsie Green with him, and we didn't see either of them for three days. Eventually, Green showed up and told us that Conley had got it into his head to go to Israel. They'd made it as far as the airport, and Conley tried to buy tickets, but neither of them even owned a passport.

Dick Stuart was a mixed blessing. A guy who hit 76 homers and 232 RBI the two years he was with the Sox, Stuart also came with some baggage; he struck out 274 times during that time. Stuart was what he was—there was no changing him, as Johnny Pesky found out. In the end, his attitude was destructive to the club, but he gave us laughs, which we sure needed. He wasn't called "Dr. Strangeglove" for nothing. The only thing that was really easy for him to catch was errors. He got an impressive 54 of them in two years. Once he mentioned that he needed to have his glove repaired. One of our wiseacres said, "Send it to a welder!"

"I know I'm the world's worst fielder," he'd say with a shrug, like it was no big thing. "But who gets paid for fielding?"

Those guys played their part in what games we won, but they didn't exactly show the stuff of champions. They ended up being symbols of the '61–'66 seasons, when we finished sixth, eighth, seventh, eighth, ninth and ninth. Of course, we also had some real pros, great players who cared about winning, guys you had to admire for showing real class even when we were so far out of first place. Guys like Pete Runnels, who won the batting championship with us in '62, just as he'd done in '60 before I came up, and hit over .300 every year he was with the club. Or Bill Monbouquette, who won 20 games for us in 1963 and anchored a starting rotation that was often adrift. Or big Dick Radatz, who threw 676 strikeouts in inning after inning of relief.

These were guys who could have made the Red Sox winners if we'd had a complete ball club. But the pieces still weren't in place, and Tom Yawkey knew it. In 1965 he decided he needed to make more changes, and he started at the top. He got rid of Higgins. That was fine with me. Higgins chain-smoked his way through salary negotiations every year, where I had to fight for every measly dollar. No matter how good a season I had, with him it was as if I was the reason we'd lost so many games. Tom replaced him at GM with Dick O'Connell, a good administrator but, more important, a guy with a vision. Working with Haywood Sullivan, who he brought in as director of player personnel, O'Connell got serious about building a new ball club. It didn't happen all at once, and it took us a year to start winning, but the road to the pennant began in the general manager's office.

The first seed of the Impossible Dream season was planted in '64, when Tony Conigliaro broke in.

I wish I could have made a splash like he did his first year: 24 homers and a .290 average. He cranked that up to 32 homers the next year, and 28 in '66. For the few fans who came to see us in those years, "Tony C.," with his Swampscott, Massachusetts, roots and his movie-star looks, became the guy to watch.

Rico Petrocelli turned into the Alex Rodriguez of his day, a shortstop who was smooth with the glove and could hit for power. Rico stuck with the club as part of the class of '65. He was a really likeable guy, but didn't have a lot of confidence in himself at first. He only became a consistent, big-league player after the Sox dumped Billy Herman and brought in Dick Williams, who then brought Eddie Popowski in just to work with Rico. Rico would end up staying with the Sox his whole career, playing fantastic baseball in two World Series.

Another piece of the dream arrived in 1965 with Jim Lonborg. Like Rico, he was a guy who was still getting seasoned during those nowhere years. Lonnie had great stuff, but his problem in '65 and '66, when he went 19-27, was that he was too damn nice. Only when he started to brush guys back and knock them down did he become a winner.

Dick O'Connell didn't bat 1.000 as GM, though. I often wondered why he didn't replace Billy Herman right away. Where Pesky had maybe been too hands-on, Herman was definitely hands-off. In fact, sometimes he seemed to care a lot more about his golf game than our baseball games. One of my first impressions of him was that he ended some of our spring training sessions early to head to the links. He talked about golf non-stop, too—in his office, the dugout, everywhere.

Under Herman the '65 season went quickly into the toilet and never made it back out, even though we'd brought in some promising young players. The team slid into seventh place in May. Funny, though—I was hot. I was hitting at a hot .350 pace. I outhit Mickey Mantle when we beat the Yankees on May 10—though to be fair to the guy he was injured.

A few nights later in Detroit I had one of my best days at the plate so far in my career—maybe ever, for that matter—when I went up against a young Denny McLain and hit for the cycle. In the second inning I ripped a second, two-run, opposite-field homer for good measure and finished the day with five RBI out of our eight runs. Unfortunately, the Tigers had twelve. We'd taken an 8-8 tie into tenth, when they hit up Dick Radatz for four runs.

It's kind of an empty satisfaction to do great in a losing effort. Right there, that game was kind of like my whole first six years.

The next night was another turning point in my '65 season—one of the turning points in my whole career to that point, actually. But it isn't one I like to think about. Late in the game I was sliding hard into second base when I took Tigers second baseman Jake Wood's knee in the ribs. I made it off the field, got a once-over in the clubhouse and was sent home. If 1965 locker rooms had the kind of medical equipment they do now, they'd have seen what I found out the next night when I passed blood: I had a damaged kidney and two broken ribs.

The pain and bleeding were so bad I couldn't move for a week. I just lay there in my hospital bed, looking at the ceiling, hurting, wondering if I was tough enough to make it back from this, slowly going nuts. My one comfort in all this—and it was a big one—was Mr. Yawkey. Tom Yawkey was an owner who cared deeply about his team, and about each individual player. Like a parent, he liked some more than others, of course, so I guess I was sort of a favorite son. He visited me every day for the nine days I was in the hospital, staying with me for hours. We cemented a deep friendship that would last until he passed away eleven years later.

Mr. Yawkey just talked to me, which was exactly what I needed to take my mind off the pain. We talked together about absolutely everything. About growing up on the farm, hunting and fishing and other things we both liked doing, and of course about baseball.

He told me, almost like it was some special secret that no one would ever know, how badly he wanted to win a pennant. Though he'd come close a few times in the '40s, when Ted Williams was at the top of his game, the only year he'd won it was 1946. And he wanted another one.

"I know one guy can't win a pennant," I said to him, "but I want to help you get one. We've got some good-looking rookies, and more kids developing in the farm system. The team will jell, I know it will. And I want to be there when it does."

They were nice thoughts to share in a heart-to-heart talk. But in 1965 it seemed like a dream. An impossible dream.

It was the best of times, it was the worst of times. Somebody said that, and I know just what he meant. He may not have been talking about the 1961-1966 Red Sox, exactly, but he could have been. That stretch produced some of the darkest days for the Fenway Faithful, and the lowest points in my career. But those low points gave me the stuff I'd need to help the club in the great years that came after.

Take the injuries. 1965 was a pretty bad year for my body, sure. But I came back. I came back from a damaged kidney and broken ribs. After I got out of the hospital, I was hitting .340 and leading the league in hitting as if nothing had happened. Then before the All-Star break I tore a leg muscle—again running for second base—and missed a lot more games. And again I came back, finishing the year at .312 and just missing the AL batting title.

You can't buy that kind of experience. I proved to myself—and my teammates—that I was tough. I gained a lot of confidence. I felt like I had the stuff to go the distance,

(TOP) JIM LONBORG HAD THE RIGHT STUFF.
(BOTTOM) RICO PETROCELLI HAD GREAT GLOVE AS WELL AS GREAT BAT.

TONY CONIGLIARO WAS A HUGE SOURCE OF PRIDE TO FENWAY FANS

whatever the distance turned out to be.

In fact, that whole sad losing period for the Red Sox—the ninth-place finishes and the jaundice, too—all of that made me emotionally tough. It taught me to play my game the best I could no matter what was happening around me. In its weird way, those years got all of us ready to go through the tightest pennant race in history. Maybe we just wanted it more than the other guys.

One of my religious-minded friends told me once it was like the Sox had to wander in the desert before they could get to the Promised Land.

I'm getting ahead of myself, though, because it was still 1965 and we weren't out of the desert yet.

After making my way back from my injuries, there was one more great memory to that season—Charlie O. Finley's Kansas City A's, who in those days were a lot better at promotional stunts than they were at winning, brought back the legendary Satchel Paige for one game. It was Paige's first major league game in twelve years. How old was he? 59? 60? "Age is a question of mind over matter," Satchel liked to say. "If you don't mind, it doesn't matter."

I'd think about that when I was in my forties, on days when I found myself playing the Wall.

Oh, yeah: in three innings, we got one measly hit off him—from yours truly.
The A's should have kept Paige in the game. We clobbered their reliever, Don Mossi, and won the game 5-3.

1966 saw O'Connell and Haywood fitting a few more pieces into our puzzle. George Scott broke in that year and had an immediate impact, tying a record by playing in every game at first base. And he was no Dr. Strangeglove, either. Boomer was the best defensive first baseman we had had since I'd been with the club, a Gold Glover. He could stretch out for throws and scoop bad ones from the dirt that Dick Stuart wouldn't even have bent over for. Not to mention that he also hit 27 homers for us his rookie year. But for me his real value was in the spirit he brought to the club. He was a fun, flashy, upbeat guy and a really aggressive competitor. He told a reporter once that the shells on his necklace were made from the teeth of second basemen.

Joe Foy, who would cover third base for us during our pennant run, also came up that year. Joe added some nice hustle in the infield and added to our home run power.

One personnel change that rubbed me the wrong way was when Billy Herman got rid of my buddy Chuck Schilling. He'd never really made it back from the doghouse after he broke his wrist under Pesky, even though he played errorless first base and drove in lots of runs. But that, like they say, is baseball.

But O'Connell got rid of Herman after he guided the team to another ninth-place finish, 27 games out of first. Now he could go play all the golf he wanted to.

Herman left a nasty legacy, though: trade rumors. He thought I wasn't hustling—at least that's what he said. I think he just knew I didn't respect him. But he told the press that he was going to trade me. Now he was gone, but the story had a life of its own. I couldn't pick up a newspaper or listen to a sports show without "the Yaz trade" being discussed. I started to take the rumors seriously and got ready to move. I tried to analyze the rumors, maybe even rationalize them. Well, they'd been paying me all kinds of money, but I hadn't hit more than 20 home runs and 94 RBI. I'd won a batting title and two Gold Gloves, but overall I was good, not great. Was I worth the highest salary on the team? Well, the Red Sox were a losing club. We were stuck in ninth place and had had as many managers in the past few years as some other teams had pennants. Maybe it'd be better to start afresh somewhere else.

Not that I wanted to. This was the only big league team I'd ever known. I owned a house in Lynnfield. I was really getting to love Boston, Fenway, the crazy fans, all of it. It felt like home.

The thing about me is that I'm a worrier. I get wrapped up in things. My hitting, the Wall, trade rumors. And I kept worrying until January, when Dick O'Connell called me into his office. He wanted to talk about two things.

"Yaz, you've got all the talent in the world. Why can't we get more out of you?"

That surprised me. I told him I'd been working on my conditioning and that I expected to have a much better year.

"That sounds good, but it's not what I'm talking about. You worry too much, Yaz. You worry about the other ballplayers, you worry about the manager, you worry about the front office, the whole damn club. Forget all that! Go out and play left field. That's your job.

MANAGER DICK WILLIAMS LIGHTENED THE MOOD.

Red Sox
TEAM

Carl Yastrzemski
PLAYER

05
CHAPTER NO.

103

Give it 100%, leave it all out there, then take a shower, go home and forget it. Anything else, that's for the manager to worry about—that's for us to worry about. Not you. OK?"

"OK," I said. Now, I knew myself. I knew I wasn't going to be able to just "take a shower, go home and forget it." Most of the time when I was eating dinner with my family my mind was miles away, going over an at bat for the twentieth time. But his general point was a good one. I was just looking forward to playing for a manager who could do a good enough job that I could relax and do mine.

"Speaking of which," O'Connell said, "about those trade rumors. We're not trading you. Mr. Yawkey told you he wouldn't trade you. Read all the newspapers you want, listen to all the radio shows you want, but don't worry, all right?"

I left the office feeling like I'd had a weight lifted off my shoulders. It was the best meeting with a GM I'd ever had. The main thing was knowing they had no intention of trading me, but to top it off O'Connell had even agreed to my salary request without an argument.

O'Connell had introduced our new manager, Dick Williams, at the end of the '66 season. I knew Dick pretty well—in fact, he had been a teammate just a couple of years before, under Pesky. Since then he'd spent a couple years managing successfully in the minors, with the old Toronto Maple Leafs of the International League. My initial thought, like everyone's, I think, was that, yeah, he could be OK. At least I didn't see an immediate, glaring problem, like golf clubs leaning against his desk. I knew he was smart, serious and a straight shooter. The team had seen three managers, though, in about that many years. So we weren't going to throw flowers at the guy. We'd wait and see how he ran the team.

Since I'd graduated from Merrimack College in the winter, I didn't have to rush off to class as soon as the 1966 baseball season ended. It was a great feeling. I couldn't remember the last time I wasn't either packing my family in the Impala and driving west to South Bend or speeding off to Merrimack right after a game. I decided I'd use the time to do what I should have been doing all along: working out and getting ready for the season ahead.

I mentioned that one day while talking with some friends at the Colonial Country Club, not far from my home in Lynnfield. They insisted I meet Gene Berde right away. Berde (pronounced "birdie") had coached the Hungarian boxing team, they said, as they walked me through the club's training room.

I don't know what I was expecting as they described him to me. I guess someone about 6'4", with bulging biceps, a tiny waist and a big black moustache. So I was initially a little disappointed at the little old guy, barely 5'6", they eventually brought me to.

"Big shot, huh?" he said in a thick Hungarian accent. "Yastrzemski, the beeeg American baseball player, Mr. Big Champion. Well, in my country, you no athlete. Look at you! I bet you not even run one mile!" He poked at my stomach. I think he would have spat if the club rules had allowed it.

"OK, you, I get you in shape. It will be hard..." he raised an eyebrow and took a long, skeptical look at me, "but I get you in shape."

He wasn't kidding. It was hard.

He put me through a nonstop fifteen-minute set of calisthenics. He was doing everything right with me, but barely broke a sweat. I was almost dead.

He looked over at me.

"You're soft, Mr. Baseball Player! Flabby! You got a lot of work to do!"

At the end of the session I said I'd be back the next day and crawled out of there. I surprised him—and myself—when I actually did come back. And I kept coming back, punching the speed bag, jumping rope, lifting weights, swinging a bat and running around the building in the snow. Berde never gave me a break between one thing and the next.

"Chin yourself!"

"Climb a rope!"

"Swing the bat!"

"OK! Outside! Run! Let's go!"

He was merciless. But after six weeks of this, six days a week, I felt like a different man. I had confidence, endurance, better coordination and motor control, and I felt like I was faster. Definitely quicker. I felt...like an athlete. I felt like I was ready.

I didn't know what for, precisely, but I was ready.

"You're not hitting enough home runs, Yaz."

When Ted Williams says that to you, you listen. It was March 1965, our last spring training in Scottsdale before the Red Sox moved their spring training camp to

Red Sox
TEAM

Carl Yastrzemski
PLAYER

CHAPTER NO.

105

Winter Haven, Florida.

"You've got no business settling for sixteen, seventeen home runs a season. You ought to be getting twice as many, with your ability and strength."

"Well, uh, how do you just become a home run hitter?" I asked him. It was like he had said I wasn't tall enough, that I should be 6'2" instead of 5'11".

"You have to pull. Not just sometimes, not just when it happens naturally. That's what's going on with you now. Instead, pull purposely. Turn your hips and shoulders away from the pitcher. That lets you pivot better and get more power into your swing."

I got back in the cage and picked up a bat. It felt strange when I tried it. It didn't feel natural. It didn't feel right.

"Work on it, Yaz. It won't come overnight. It may not even happen this season. But it'll happen. Keep working on it."

In '65, despite the injuries, I hit 20 home runs. Come spring training '66, Williams wasn't impressed.

"For a guy like you, 20 homers is beans. You lack confidence. Now close your hips. Show the pitcher more of your tail. Use your power."

It was too much of a stretch. I couldn't get myself into the stance he wanted. But in '66 I couldn't find my old swing either. I was neither here nor there—and my average sank, and I didn't even get as many home runs as the year before. I had to do something.

I realized that Williams was right. And that I'd been resisting him. It was time to take my game to the next level.

When I hit spring training in 1967, the first thing I did was find Ted Williams. I didn't even say hello.

"You say I can become a home run hitter, Ted. Well, OK. Now I'm ready." **8**

Red Sox
TEAM

Carl Yastrzemski
PLAYER

0 5
CHAPTER NO.

107

ALI & DUNDEE Part 2

Sports Illustrated
AUGUST 21, 1967   40 CENTS

RED SOX SLUGGER
CARL YASTRZEMSKI

Red Sox
TEAM

Carl Yastrzemski
PLAYER

06
CHAPTER NO.

109

THE IMPOSSIBLE DREAM

Yankee Stadium, Opening Day, April 14, 1967

I t was a pretty thin crowd as we took on Whitey Ford and the Yankees in their home opener. They'd only finished in eighth place last year, but they were still the Yankees. Mickey Mantle, Joe Pepitone, Elston Howard, Tom Tresh. You didn't take them lightly.

Billy Rohr didn't. He was a 20-year-old lefty making his very first major league start. The night before the game he had kept Jim Lonborg up half the night asking him over and over again about the Yankee hitters. He looked pretty damn shaky on the bus.

Reggie Smith, our rookie center fielder, gave Rohr something to work with by leading the game off with a solo homer. And once Rohr threw his first pitch in the bottom of the inning, he was all business. He retired Clarke, Robinson and Tresh. Third inning, same thing. Inning after inning he was setting them down in order. He'd walk a few here and there, but leave 'em stranded. People started to get what they might be seeing—you heard some murmurs from the stands. We started moving away from him on the bench.

You don't talk to a guy when he's pitching a no-hitter.

In the sixth inning Rohr had a couple of close calls. Horace Clarke hit a flare to left that looked like it might drop for a base hit. But I got a good jump, ran in at full sprint and grabbed it. The next batter gave Rohr a scare—and his first assist. Bill Robinson, the Yankees' right fielder, hit a hard grounder up the middle right that caromed off Rohr's shin to Joe Foy at third. Foy threw to Scott at first for the out. Dick Williams rushed out with our trainer, Buddy LeRoux, but Rohr shook it off.

Foy gave Rohr a three-run lead with a two-run homer in the eighth. By the time Rohr came to the mound, even the dimmest fans in the stands were sitting up and taking notice. There's no tension quite like no-hitter tension, and it was everywhere. Ralph Houk started off their half of the inning by sending in Mickey Mantle as a pinch hitter for the shortstop, Kennedy. People applauded for Mantle—you always applauded for the Mick—but they liked it even better when he flied out to Conigliaro in right.

The Yankee fans hated the Sox, always, but today they were on Rohr's side.

Lou Clinton reached on a throwing error and then Rohr walked Clarke. But he pulled himself together and got Robinson to ground into a double play.

Billy Rohr was three outs from a no-hitter.

In the bottom of the ninth, before he threw his first pitch to Tresh, the crowd rose and gave the kid a standing ovation. Rohr looked around the infield, out to the fielders and the Yankee fans in the stands, soaking it in. And we Red Sox all looked right back at him. We all wanted that no-hitter for him as much as he wanted it for himself. Even the Yankee fans in left were saying, "Hey Yaz, help the kid out! Don't let anybody get a hit offa him!"

Rohr started working to Tresh and got to a full count. I was playing a bit shallow, probably shallower than I should have been. Tresh was still a home run threat. On the other hand, when a guy's got a no-hitter going, you don't want a hit to dribble out of the infield, either.

And then it happened. Tresh connected on the 3-2 pitch. The ball flew into deep left, deep, deep...everybody in the stadium must have been thinking, "Awww, there goes the kid's no-hitter...it's way over Yastrzemski's head...there's no way he's ever gonna get that..."

I didn't think anything. I just turned my back to the plate and ran.

I knew the ball was going to stay in. But could I get to it? Running at full tilt, running like Berde was yelling in my ear, I looked up. The ball was coming down fast now, and coming down ahead of where I was. There was only one way I could have a chance in hell of getting it. I dove. I dove, my cap flew off, I stretched my glove out, my arm, my whole body...and—*chunk*—felt it in the webbing. I got it!

My left knee hit the ground and I went into a somersault, but I held on to the damn thing. Rohr's no-hitter was still alive.

The crowd went wild.

Yankee fans? Applauding my catch? *Where was I?*

Joe Pepitone flied out on the next pitch. People were stamping and cheering. But for Rohr! They wanted their guys to get outs, not hits. Dick Williams went out to the mound to talk things over with Rohr as Elston Howard came up.

Howard swung at Rohr's first pitch, low and away. After four more pitches, he'd run the count full. But then, on what Rohr told me later had been a curveball that didn't break, Howard blooped over Mike Andrews's head into right center. A base hit. Boos and catcalls filled the park. Later on, Howard was defensive about getting a hit in his own ballpark. It was that kind of day—and it would be that kind of season. Crazy.

Charlie Smith, the next guy up, flied out on Rohr's first pitch to end the game.

We ran in and mobbed Rohr. The kid had lost his no-hitter, but he'd won a place in history. Red Sox history, at least.

We were a club that had lost 535 games over the last six years, a lot of them because of spotty pitching, many of them because we just plain underperformed. So a win like this on opening day, against the Yankees, no less, was electrifying. At the time, you didn't want to read too much into it. It's a long season, after all, and so many other seasons had gone south on us. Like they say, though, hope springs eternal. Especially for the Red Sox. Every year, it looked like we had put the pieces in place in the spring. And every year, we'd think, well, maybe this year...

Well...why *not* this year?

With the kind of season we had in 1967, coming on top of the seasons that had led up to it, it's so natural to look back and say, "Oh, change was in the air!" The more realistic way to look at it is, "Who knew?"

Getting the pennant? That was crazy talk.

But there was change in the air. Outside baseball, America was going through an incredible transformation. You had young people speaking up, questioning things. Protests about the Vietnam War were beginning. The civil rights movement was shaking

MAKING A DIVING CATCH IS ONE OF THE GREATEST PLEASURES IN THE WORLD.

things up in the South and everywhere else. The music, the styles, the long hair…all those things are just part of the way America is now, but it's hard to imagine the impact it all had on the country at the time. All assumptions went out the window. The message was, why not do things in a whole new way?

In sports, football was starting to challenge baseball as America's game. Although it wasn't even called the Super Bowl yet, the National Football League played the American Football League for the first time that year in a "World Championship Game." In boxing, heavyweight champion Muhammad Ali, someone who always did the unexpected, made a big political statement by refusing to go into the army and fight in Vietnam.

In baseball, Curt Flood's challenge to the reserve clause that started free agency was still two years away. So in a lot of ways, it was business as usual. You were basically owned by your team, and spring training was still hard work and sore muscles.

Dick Williams was everywhere as we trained in Winter Haven, Florida, for the first time. He watched everything, looked at everyone and didn't take anything for granted. He oversaw infield drills and looked hard at the vets in the batting cage. He even put on a mask and played umpire. And guys argued with him like he was the real thing.

There were rules, a schedule you had to follow, and Williams enforced all of it. It was intense, too. We worked harder than we ever had in a spring training. There was no walking through the drills—they were serious. He wanted to see results. When it came time to run, he made sure you were running. He made the pitchers play volleyball to stay in shape.

After Herman, I was happy to see all of that. Williams was on top of everything, but he had a lot more control, somehow, than Pesky did. You had the sense that Williams knew where he wanted to take the team.

I was also happy about some of the rookies who had joined the club. Two in particular: Reggie Smith and Mike Andrews. Even with all the great additions of the past couple of years—Conigliaro, Petrocelli, Scott, Foy—we were still weak up the middle. Reggie was a great hitter—he could homer from either side of the plate—and a great fielder in Fenway's deep center. Mike added some snap in the bat from the second baseman's spot, something we didn't have before.

Sometimes I'd just stand there looking at all these guys. It was the best collection of baseball talent we'd had since I'd joined the club. The odds didn't look great on paper,

I'll admit—we'd finished ninth or near there too many years in a row. Vegas had us at 100-1 to make the pennant. I don't think the fans, except maybe in some deep, irrational place in their hearts, expected much better. But this was a young team. There wasn't a Dick Stuart in the bunch. Guys were too young not to hustle, too inexperienced to be cynical and too smart to think they knew more than the manager. They were also too naïve to know they weren't supposed to win it all. Our new manager was smart, and serious about his business. Maybe, just maybe, we could be the Red Sox without being like...the Red Sox.

I made the most of my spring training. I felt strong and conditioned when I arrived, for the first time, thanks to Berde. And I looked for Williams right away, practically grabbed the guy, and told him I was ready—really ready—to be a pull hitter, the home run hitter I was supposed to be.

He looked down at me and smiled, like he'd been waiting for me to say that.

THE 1967 RED SOX OUTFIELD, YASTRZEMSKI, SMITH AND CONIGLIARO

"Fine. Well, sounds like you are ready now. You weren't before—that was the problem. Okay, listen, Yaz, it's all in the hips. That's where the secret of hitting homers is."

He gave me his lecture about how to turn your hips away from the pitcher, use them for leverage so you can bring more power to your swing without changing it. I had heard it before, but now it was as if I was hearing it for the first time. I spent as much time as I could that spring working on it, with him watching.

I started seeing results right away, hitting homers in exhibition games against both right- and left-handed pitching. Southpaws had always mixed me up, but I hit two homers against the Cardinals' lefty Al Jackson.

I was looking forward to blasting them out of the park when the regular season opened. It didn't happen, though. In fact, I wasn't hitting much at all, with only two homers at the beginning of May. And the whole team was dragging right with me. By May 13 we had fallen to sixth place and were below .500, losing eight out of the last ten. Trying to get us out of the slump, Dick Williams even benched me for a while. My power was there, but the results weren't.

I went to Bobby Doerr, our batting coach. He put me in the cage, looked at my swing and suggested I hold the bat higher.

"Maybe as high as your left ear," he said. I raised my arms almost to where they'd been before, when I'd been unconsciously imitating Musial. But now, with Berde's training to give me strength and Ted Williams's coaching to show me how to pull, it felt like it was all coming together. I whacked the next pitch, and the next, and the next. I was striking the ball level now, but with power.

I know Williams's first words to me were "Never let 'em screw with your swing," but I was notorious for tinkering with it myself. I was never satisfied with my performance, rarely even satisfied with individual at bats. I'm always trying to find the right formula—always reaching for perfection.

We were playing the Tigers in a doubleheader that day. Denny McLain was pitching. I stepped to the plate. I raised my bat high like Doerr had suggested, turned my hips like Williams had showed me and ripped McLain's fastball into the bleachers in center field using all the power Berde had packed into me over the winter. In the second game of the day, I knocked another one out. I finished the doubleheader by going three for eight, with three RBI and four runs. Not too shabby. Even I felt pretty good about that.

Coincidentally or not, the Sox moved out of our slump. We put together a four-game winning streak at the end of May, beating the Orioles, the Angels and the Twins and crawling over .500. I figured in the league leader columns in batting, homers and RBI, trailing only the Tigers' Al Kaline in batting and the previous year's Triple Crown winner, Frank Robinson, in homers and RBI. What was important to me, though, was that I had 10 homers and 30 RBI. All the work was paying off. I was on my way to my real goal of helping the team score runs and win games.

The thing that hung over us like a sword, though, was our pitching. If anything had done in the promising teams we'd had in the past six years, that was it.

We only had one reliable right-hander on the staff, and that was Jim Lonborg.

Lonnie had always looked good on the mound, but only had a measly 27-19 career record to show for it. Great guy, smart, went to Stanford, listened to classical music, for Pete's sake. His problem was that he seemed to lack competitive fire. They called him

BATTING COACH BOBBY DOERR WAS INVALUABLE TO ME IN 1967

"Gentleman Jim." That's no name for a pitcher! In the 1967 season, though, he caught fire. He became aggressive. Really aggressive—throwing at guys, knocking them down, never giving up on games. June 21 we were playing the Yankees, beating them 4-0 when their starter, Thad Tillotson, beaned Joe Foy, who had hit a grand slam off them the night before. Plunked him right on the helmet. Dick Williams folded his arms and stared out at Foy jogging to first base.

"We know what we've got to do," he muttered.

Lonborg heard him. When Tillotson came up to bat in the second (this was before the days of the DH, and AL pitchers hit for themselves), Lonnie knocked him in the shoulder with his big fastball. As Tillotson ran to first he yelled over to Lonborg: "You're gonna be up again!"

Foy moved over from third and started jawing at Tillotson.

"If you're thinking of starting something you're going to have to go through me!" he shouted. That's when all hell pretty much broke loose.

It was an epic brawl. Rico Petrocelli's left hook knocked Yankee first baseman Joe Pepitone out of the game, but nobody was ejected.

Lonnie wasn't done, though—and neither was Tillotson. Tillotson knocked Lonborg down in the third, clearing the benches again, and in the bottom of the inning Lonnie brushed back Charlie Smith and then slammed Dick Howser in the back. The dugouts emptied for the third time.

I think it was Dick Williams who lit the fire under Lonnie that year—not just in that one game. And even the brawl, that new Red Sox fighting spirit, might have been a reflection of Williams's hard-nosed style. Yeah, we'd had our share of brawls in the past six seasons. And there was always a lot of hostility towards the Yankees. But this was different. Guys were sticking up for each other, defending each other. We were playing as a team, fighting for something together. Sometimes literally.

Dick Williams was not what you'd call a sweet guy. Off the field he was perfectly decent—a very fair man. But when it came to baseball he only cared about one thing: winning. And he didn't have time to baby anyone. If it meant screaming at you, benching you

Red Sox
TEAM

Carl Yastrzemski
PLAYER

CHAPTER NO.

119

or even knocking you in the press, he'd do it. I didn't always agree with him—we knocked heads on a few occasions, like the time he put down George Scott to a reporter. "Talking to Scott is like talking to a cement wall," he said. He was constantly after Scott and Foy about their weight—he benched Boomer over it and told the newspapers that Foy was so fat he couldn't bend over for a ground ball. In May, he screamed at Lonborg after Jim lost a no-hitter in the ninth on a wild pitch. But Williams got results. With both his bat and his glove, Scott ended up being a big part of our success that year. Lonnie won 22 games and got 245 strikeouts for us, marking his glove with batters he hit like an American fighter ace painting little rising suns or iron crosses on his plane.

That Yankees game eventually ended more or less peacefully, and Lonborg came out on top. The win gave him a 9-2 record. In games where he wasn't part of the decision, though, we were 24-29. We needed another arm. And this year, management was looking out for us. O'Connell and Haywood weren't just pushing pencils up there—they wanted to win, too. In June, they dealt for Gary Bell, giving us another right-handed stopper. Gary was 12-8 with us that season.

They also brought in Jerry Adair, a talented utility infielder who batted .291 in '67. I thought getting him showed some ESP in the front office, because shortly after he arrived Rico Petrocelli went down with a wrist injury. That could have been a real blow to the team, but Adair stepped in at short, played great defense and actually bumped up the team batting average.

Things seemed to be going along OK with the All-Star break in sight, but then we stumbled and fell into a five-game losing streak. We had to close out the first half of the season with a win. We'd fallen to fifth place, behind the White Sox, Tigers, Twins and Angels, so we couldn't afford to slip any further.

The last day before the break, July 9, was a doubleheader. Tiger Stadium was a steam bath that day. We dropped the first game behind Gary Bell. That left us only the second game to close out the first half of the season as winners.

If we lost, we'd be at .500 again. Even more than that, we wanted to win to keep the momentum going and our spirits high. Lonborg, who was sweating even before his first pitch, hurled seven tough shutout innings to get the win—losing 12 lbs. to dehydration in the process. Wyatt made a nice save, and I broke out of a mini slump with five hits between the two games. I got a homer in the eighth inning of the second as insurance to

Red Sox
TEAM

Carl Yastrzemski
PLAYER

CHAPTER NO.

121

seal Lonnie's victory and send myself into my second All-Star game in Anaheim with some All-Star pizzazz.

It was actually the third time I'd been elected to the Game. I'd gone in 1963 (though I hadn't done much), but in 1966 I was injured. This year I made up for lost time, getting three hits and three walks, but the Americans came up short. It was an indication of the kind of year we were having that Rico Petrocelli, Tony Conigliaro and Jim Lonborg were sent to the Game, too.

Every day of the Impossible Dream season counted in that crazy, you-won't-believe-this story, even from O'Connell's appointment of Dick Williams at the end of the last season through the tough spring training regimen and right up to the neck-and-neck finish. But the really wild, fever-dream part of it started after the All-Star break. When we all started playing beyond ourselves, when the balls started falling our way and all of us, even our fans, felt like we were being swept along by something bigger than ourselves.

We got back to playing with a doubleheader, and a win, taking the first game from the Orioles with all the offense we needed coming in a three-run first inning. We dropped the nightcap, but came back to Fenway the next day ready for more.

That day, July 17, 1967, was the day things really started to take off—like the Conigliaro homer that zoomed out of the park and cleared the left field fence in our 11-5 stomping of Baltimore. In the final game against Baltimore we kept things from getting out of hand in the very first inning with a triple play, and we ran our little streak to four and leapfrogged from fifth place to third in a two-game getaway series against Detroit. Then we hit the road briefly and took four straight against Cleveland, where Tony C. and I each hit two more home runs.

We had just put together a ten-game sweep. Nobody could remember the last time that had happened. We were in second place, half a game behind the White Sox. Everybody was happy and excited.

People had been thinking, yeah, the Sox are having a nice season so far. But then they realized that maybe it was more than just a nice season. For players and fans alike, the Sox were getting to be like Rohr's performance on Opening Day; comes a certain point, you realize he's not just having a nice game—he's pitching a no-hitter.

As we flew home from Cleveland, the pilot came on the intercom and told us something was happening at Logan Airport, there were some people waiting for us. I

I WAS A REAL STICKLER ABOUT FUNDAMENTALS, LIKE RUNNING STRAIGHT DOWN THE FIRST BASE LINE ON EVERY CONTACT

was only half aware of the announcement at the time. When we actually had to land on a different runway, though, we all realized it wasn't just a few wives and girlfriends who'd come to meet us.

The tarmac was swarming with 15,000 Red Sox fans.

Because they'd made the plane park so far away, we boarded buses to get to the terminal. The fans surrounded us. I stood up and asked, "Does anybody know if they're hostile?"

I was only half joking. This kind of reception was as confusing as Yankee fans booing Elston Howard for getting a base hit. The crowd on the tarmac was a lot bigger than the attendance at a lot of our home games had been for years.

The fans rushed the bus, squeezing around it, pressing their faces to the windows. They started rocking the thing back and forth. We couldn't even get off. It was bizarre, it was new, it was scary, it was great. We looked at each other with wide eyes.

We came into August holding a 56-44 record. We still trailed the White Sox, now by two games. The Tigers, in third place, were two games behind us, and the Twins and Angels both were another game behind them. We stumbled through the first part of the month, playing only about .333 ball. We weren't discouraged, though. By now we were believers.

It helped, too, that we were already getting a preview of the crazy, close finish that season was going to have. Despite losing twice as many games as we won, we kept pace. Even though we slipped to fifth at one point, we were never more than two and a half games out.

Dick Williams defined himself during August, I thought. On the one hand, he never lost confidence, never seemed to lose the vision of where we were going and what we needed to get there. He called up Dave Morehead, a right-handed pitcher who'd been bouncing around the Sox system for the past few years. He also worked with O'Connell and Sullivan to give us an element of pennant race and post-season experience, and he dealt for Howard, who at 38 had been a fixture behind the plate for the Yankees forever, it seemed, and was about the best guy at calling games I ever saw.

On the other hand, though, he was so fixed on that vision that he lost us games, on purpose, just to prove a point.

The George Scott incident was a good example. Boomer was a big guy who had a tendency to get bigger. Williams told him unless he met a weight target of 211 he wasn't going to play. With a crucial mid-August series coming up against the Angels, Boomer stepped on the scale. 220. Dick had laid down the law—and he wasn't going to back away, even though it would probably hurt us not to have Scott in the lineup.

Scott sat and sulked—and we lost all three games.

But the point Williams felt he needed to make, even at the expense of slipping in the standings, was that everyone needed to have commitment, focus and discipline if we were going to be able to win the pennant. And if they didn't, they'd be riding the pine like Boomer.

In late August we started winning again, putting together a seven-game winning streak—but at a terrible cost.

Friday, August 18. It was the Angels at Fenway. Jack Hamilton was their spitball specialist. Tony Conigliaro, one of the only guys who was having any success against him, came to the plate in the fourth. Tony was an aggressive young guy who acted like he wasn't afraid of anything. He'd crowd the plate, forcing the pitcher to give him a good ball to hit. Hamilton, on the other hand, was an aggressive pitcher who wasn't going to concede any part of the plate. It was the immovable object versus the irresistible force.

That night, the force won. Hamilton's first pitch came at head level. Tony didn't flinch until everyone in the park heard the pop of a baseball against bone and flesh.

Tony went down immediately. Blood was rushing from his nose and his left eye was a swollen, black mess.

Rico ran over to him from the on-deck circle and crouched over him, whispering, "You're gonna be OK. It's gonna be fine." But as Tony lay there his legs were kicking out on the ground like he was a man being tortured.

It didn't look like it was gonna be fine.

We received conflicting reports over the next few days: he'd be back in a month, next year, his career was over. Eventually, Tony did come back to the Red Sox, but it wasn't until 1969.

We were all shaken up—the whole crowd was shaken up, just seeing and hearing that injury to someone, much less a handsome, young, local guy who had one of your

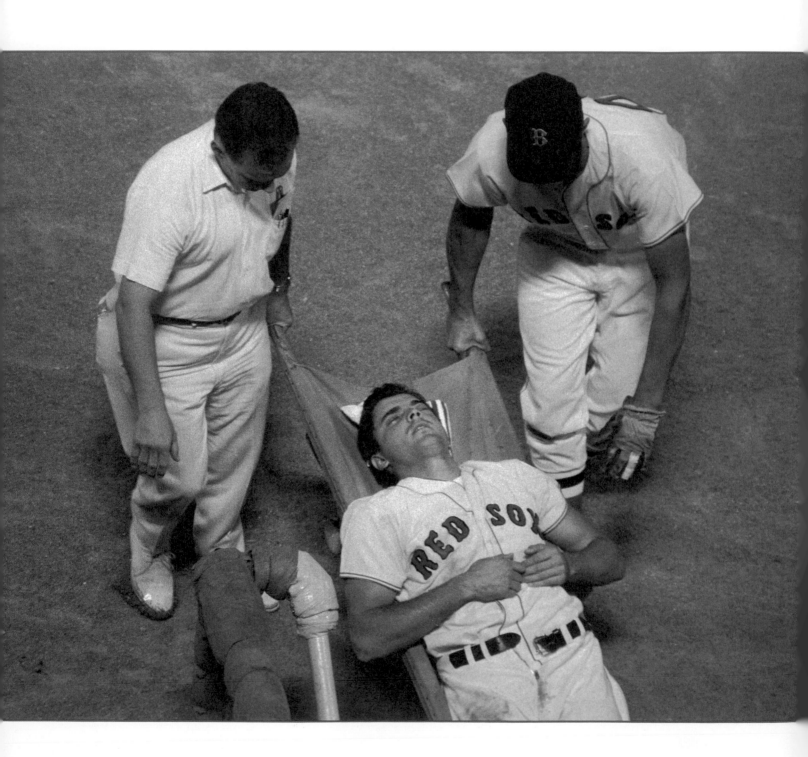

Red Sox
TEAM

Carl Yastrzemski
PLAYER

0 6
CHAPTER NO.

125

TONY CONIGLIARO DEFINED COURAGE.

hottest bats. Tony had hit 20 homers so far that year, and driven in 67 runs. We ended pulling out a win for him that day—barely.

Tony's story crossed that happy season with its saddest note. I never played with a guy with more potential, and in one sickening moment, it was gone. Tony was the youngest player ever to reach 100 home runs. Who knows how much further he could have gone with us that season and the ones that followed? Tony C. had that movie-star flash to him, too—a great baseball career might have been just a step along the way to something even bigger. Though he made his way back from the injury and was the Comeback Player of the Year two seasons later, vision problems caught up with him and he retired in 1971. Ten years after that, Tony suffered a heart attack, which left him with debilitating brain damage. He died in 1990. He was just 45 years old.

The day after Tony went down we creamed the Angels in the opening game of a doubleheader, 12-2, but got into trouble early in the second game, with Hamilton pitching again. After the second inning, they were leading 8-0. Then Reggie homered, I crunched one to right and the fans started lighting into Hamilton for what he'd done to Tony C. He started losing control, walking batters, and eventually got blown off the mound by tornado-force Fenway boos. Our batters were equally relentless, and we clawed our way back from an 8-0 deficit to a 9-8 victory. I'm no baseball historian, but I can't remember when that was done before.

It seemed like unbelievable, stranger-than-fiction wins like this were becoming business as usual for us. But that's how it is in a pennant race. Funny things happen. It's hard not to feel like destiny is playing a part in the whole thing.

We went on to take seven in a row. We stayed within a game of the White Sox the whole time, but just couldn't seem to overtake them.

On August 25 we finally got a chance to go to Chicago and face the White Sox. It was a particularly hostile series, not only because of the half game that separated us, but also because their manager, Eddie Stanky, was one of the most dislikable characters in professional baseball. In the first game of our opening doubleheader, I had already gotten three hits when Stanky put in a left-hander, Wilbur Wood, to do just one thing: hit me. Pitches were going by my head, behind me. I felt as if I were in a western movie. Eventually Wood ran out of chances to plunk me and I walked. We dropped the afternoon contest, but won the next day to take first place.

Red Sox
TEAM

Carl Yastrzemski
PLAYER

0 6
CHAPTER NO.

127

I'd never been in first place in August with the club since I'd broken in, so I had to check with someone to find out the last time it had happened: 1959. After the game, I asked to take BP. Stanky said yes—and then made me wait until it was almost dark while he walked his poodle, Go-Go, through the outfield.

We split that doubleheader—and then another one, two days after. We beat them the Saturday in between, though, which kept us in first. Our road trip took us to New York, with me in a 0-17 slump. We played yet another doubleheader against the Yankees—losing a 20-inning second game. When we got back to Fenway we were exhausted, and barely holding on to first place.

What with the slump, my batting average had slipped to .308, which put me behind Frank Robinson for the batting title. I had 34 home runs, though, the most in the league, and I also led in RBI. I was barely aware of those numbers, though. The only numbers that mattered were the little ones that separated my team from Minnesota, Detroit and Chicago. On September 1 it was us, the Twins, the Tigers and the White Sox, with a slim half game between each of us. And it actually wasn't as simple as half games. It came down to percentage points. For instance, over the next week we played .500 ball against the White Sox and Senators and slipped out of first by a tenth of a percentage point. .001. That was all that separated us from Minnesota.

By now it had dawned on us that A, we were probably going to be there at the end, one way or the other, but B, it was going to be tight. Very tight.

The Red Sox needed to replace Conigliaro in the lineup for the coming stretch. A big reason I had a big year was that I'd had Tony hitting behind me at cleanup—and Reggie Smith hitting in the number-two spot. Because of those guys, they couldn't pitch around me. We were lucky to pick up another big bat. Ken "Hawk" Harrelson, a flashy guy with a big mouth and a big bat, had just been released by the A's. Apparently owner Charlie O. Finley, who'd just fired manager Alvin Dark, didn't like one of his players calling him a "nut cake."

We couldn't have had the year we had without Hawk in the lineup. I loved having him around the clubhouse, too. Not only was his first at bat a home run, but he drew reporters to him like moths to a light. That meant they weren't pestering me.

I never felt particularly comfortable talking to the press. I couldn't be more differ-ent from Harrelson. I liked to let my game speak for me. I just wanted to get in there and hit, or play balls off the Wall. The unbelievable rush of hitting a game-winning homer in front of 35,000 fans was why I put in the years of hard work, swinging the heavy bat in a freezing garage and bumping along in a bus across North Carolina every day.

We left Boston for our final, eight-game road trip on Sunday, September 17, after dropping three straight to the Orioles at Fenway. The Orioles, who were in eighth place! We weren't making it easy on ourselves.

This was not a time to make mistakes. To say every game counted was a huge understatement. Every percentage point counted. And each Tigers, White Sox and Twins percentage point counted, too. We were still bunched together, all of us separated by one game, total.

Boston was going Red Sox crazy. There was a buzz around town you could light a Christmas tree with. In Fenway, we had bigger crowds than old hands had seen since Ted Williams was with the club. From the Back Bay to the North End to Roxbury and all the way up to the Quebec border, the Sox were all anyone could talk about. Someone saw a GO SOX! bumper sticker on a hearse.

I was looking forward to getting out of town for a while. It wasn't so much the fans—it was great to have them excited about the club, even the funeral directors. No, it was the wind. It had stymied left-handers lately, blowing in from right.

Fenway's got fickle winds in the autumn. Sometimes they help, sometimes they hurt.

In the first of our two games at Tiger Stadium, Dick Williams shook the order up a bit, starting Dalton Jones at third and sitting Hawk Harrelson, who'd been in a slump. The game was tied after seven and a half innings, but Detroit scored a run in the bottom half of the eighth. It was 5-4 in the bottom of the ninth when I came to the plate with one out. With a 2-0 count, Fred Lasher, one of four pitchers who'd come on that night in relief of Denny McLain, read the signs from catcher Bill Freehan, and I said a silent Hail Mary.

At this point, I was looking for situations where I could take the shot, win the game. Actually, I didn't have to look for them—they came to me. I was on some sort of weird high, in a zone that last two weeks of the season, and taking the whole team with me. I was playing the game at a higher level than I knew I had, guided in almost everything by something larger than myself.

HOME RUNS ARE PURE SATISFACTION

Hail Mary, full of grace, the Lord is with thee. Blessed art thou amongst women...

I raised my bat high. I was thinking fastball. Lasher delivered one. I crushed my 40th home run into the upper right field deck of Tiger Stadium. Suddenly, the place was silent, the only sound my footsteps in the dirt as I ran around the bases.

I'd now hit twice as many homers as my previous high. Just like Ted Williams said. But I didn't think much about it. That home run had only tied the game. We kept them from scoring in their half of the ninth, and in the tenth, Dalton Jones faced right-hander Mike Marshall. Jones, who hadn't been used much throughout the year, had hit three singles already that night. This time he banged a homer off a steel girder in the upper fight field stands. Santiago came on to close, and we had one of our most clutch wins in a year filled with them.

The next night we squeezed out another ninth-inning comeback in a tense, playoff–like game and then went on to Cleveland, where I was five for nine and hit home run number 41 in a two-game set. In Baltimore we split a doubleheader to open the four-game series. In the third game, Frank Robinson hit one out of the park, then I brought us back with number 42, then Brooks Robinson hit a two-run shot to seal it for the O's. Just like that, we were in third place.

We looked to Lonborg in the fourth game, and he didn't disappoint. We came away with an 11-7 victory, but none of those seven Baltimore runs were his. We were back in second place, but it was just a matter of percentage points. Monday, in fact, we slid back into a tie for first on a day off, with the Twins losing to the Angels.

We all took a deep breath and looked ahead to our final home stand—two games each against the Indians and the Twins. The Sox hysteria was at fever pitch. The tight pennant race had captured the nation's attention, too, what with the St. Louis Cardinals having run away with the National League pennant, and Red Sox fans were coming out of the woodwork across the U.S., and even on rival baseball teams.

I don't know what happened in our first game against Cleveland on Tuesday the 26th, but we didn't play like the house was on fire. My future teammate and friend Luis Tiant held us scoreless through six innings, while Indians manager Joe Adcock was walking me as much as he could.

"I don't think Yaz knows what pressure is, " he said. " I decided he had beaten us often enough."

But I was able to hit my 43rd home run shot in the seventh for 115 RBI, which tied me with Ted Williams for the most ever by a Red Sox lefty (Jimmie Foxx, a righty, hit 50) and lifted my average to .319, but it was too little too late. We lost, 6-3.

Meanwhile, the Twins got back at the Angels behind Harmon Killebrew's two home runs, which gave him 43, as well. And gave the Twins a one-game lead. We were tied for second with the White Sox. The Tigers were still in it, but mathematically, the pennant was the Twins' to lose. All they had to do was win two out of their last three.

It seemed like we were finally starting to self-destruct. We were tight, nervous, not having fun like we'd had for so much of the season. All the pressure was suddenly crashing down on us and we couldn't hit. Tiant pitched again, and the Indians shut us out Wednesday, 6-0.

I figured that was our season. We had had a good run, and we all accepted it and congratulated each other. Then we sat down, had ham sandwiches, drank beer and thought ahead to next season. Funny, all I was really thinking of was my parents, who had driven to a Long Island Sound beach at the height of the potato harvest so they could pick up the game on the radio.

Some news filtered into the clubhouse: the Angels had beaten the Twins. Interesting...that meant we weren't absolutely out of it, but it was unlikely. The Tigers could split their four-game series against the Angels, and the odds were with the White Sox in their doubleheaders against the A's. I went home thinking our season was as good as over.

Still, I kept checking with the Boston papers on the latest wire reports of the Chicago-Kansas City doubleheader. The Athletics led early, but then they kept leading and actually beat White Sox ace Gary Peters in the first game. Well, I figured, the A's won't be able to get by Joel Horlen. Horlen was Chicago's other stopper. But the A's countered with a 20-year-old righty named Jim "Catfish" Hunter, who blanked the White Sox on a three-hitter. Suddenly, Chicago was in fourth place. And at this stage, that effectively meant *they* were out of it.

GRANDMA, MOM AND DAD AT FENWAY FOR THE PENNANT RUN

HARMON KILLEBREW OF THE TWINS...

Red Sox
TEAM

Carl Yastrzemski
PLAYER

0 6
CHAPTER NO.

133

HOME RUN #44 COULD NOT HAVE COME AT A BETTER TIME

There was little chance the White Sox, Twins and Red Sox would have all lost in that three-day stretch. But we all did. And that's the stuff pennant races are made of.

We had an endless two-day break in our schedule before we played the Twins on Saturday. On Thursday, the Tigers and Angels were rained out in California, meaning they'd be playing a doubleheader the next day.

Friday, the Senators drove the final nail into Chicago's coffin, beating the White Sox 1-0. And the Tigers and Angels had been rained out again. The whole season was coming down to the final weekend.

Come Friday, my place in Lynnfield was packed to the rafters with Yastrzemskis and Skoniecznys. It was great to see them all, but on the other hand, I had to get out of there as soon as I could. I phoned the Colonial Inn and got a room.

I tossed and turned all night. Everything, the past leading up to this moment and the future that would come out of it, was turning on the 5'11" frame of Carl Yastrzemski Jr. I got out of bed as soon as dawn broke Saturday and walked the golf course. I thought about the Twins, the toughest opponents we'd had all year. I thought about my role and how I felt—I knew—that I'd play the pivotal role in these two games. This was my moment, my time.

But how? What would I do?

No way of knowing. I went to the park early to get warmed up. Jose Santiago was starting that day. Jose had bounced around a bit, and even this year he'd only started eleven games, pitching mostly in middle relief. But Dick Williams had him in the rotation now, and Santiago promised me that he wouldn't let Killebrew hit a home run off him.

"Jose," I said, "you stop him and I'll make sure to hit a homer for you."

The place was packed with more fans than I thought it could hold. There were 32,000 screaming Sox faithful there. Even the ones who were only just deciding we might not fold at the last minute came out of their holes in the ground. Senator Ted Kennedy was in attendance, too, and Vice President Hubert Humphrey threw out the first ball.

I guess this is a big deal, I thought to myself.

Jose and I both kept our promises to each other. In the bottom of the seventh

I came up with two runners on. Jim Merritt, a lefty, was sent in just to face me. I knew he liked to throw sliders, but with the longer right field of Fenway, I figured on a fastball. Especially when he took the count to 3-1. *Crack!* I got the sweet spot of the barrel right on it, and the ball sailed into the right field bleachers. Number 44.

Only as I circled the bases did I start to hear the deafening noise I'd been blocking out as I faced Merritt.

It was 6-2. Santiago had kept Killebrew in the park that day, but Jose was lifted in the next inning before he could face him again. In the ninth, Williams trotted out and told Gary Bell to pitch to Killebrew. We needed an out to end the game more than we needed to keep them from scoring runs. Killer jumped on Bell's fat fastball and slugged it for his 44th homer. Bell then got the next batter, Oliva, ending the game. We won, 6-4.

Lonborg beat the Twins Sunday—and then was nearly torn to pieces by out-of-their-minds-happy Sox fans. Things got a little soppy in the clubhouse. Beer, soda and shaving cream were flying around as people pounded and hugged each other. Lonnie was in the last shreds of his uniform. He, Reggie, Rico and I posed for pictures, four of the wettest, happiest guys you ever saw. There were tears, too. Tony C., who'd sat in the dugout with us during the game, was crying. Tom Yawkey shed tears when he thanked Williams for the great job he'd done. Dick and Mr. Yawkey had had their disagreements, and there would be lots more, but just then they were brought together in an incredible high no one could ever have imagined at the beginning of the season.

Mr. Yawkey had come over to my locker and put me in a big bear hug a few moments earlier. He was barely able to choke out, "I don't know how to thank you."

"Don't even try, Mr. Yawkey," I said. Now I was almost crying, too. I'd wanted to give him this victory for years now. "You and I are the only ones left who really understand what this means, you know?"

He nodded.

"You're the last survivor, Yaz, the only one left from the bad years from 1961. Now you're the old man here," he laughed. "You and me."

Yup, pretty soppy. And now Mr. Yawkey's shirt and suit were soaked from hugging me, with flecks of shaving cream on his tie. But there wasn't any champagne yet.

Because we actually hadn't won anything.

The Tigers were still alive, and still playing their final doubleheader against the Angels. They'd beaten California in the first game, 6-4. And as we were jumping up and down and spraying each other, they started winning the second one. If they hung on, it'd mean a play-off.

The game wasn't on TV. In a sign of America's changing tastes, NBC had decided to switch to an AFL game with the Raiders and Chiefs. We brought a little radio out of the trainer's room. Ernie Harwell, the Tigers' announcer, was calling the game in his deep, old-time voice. The beer started to dry on our clothes, the shaving cream dissolved and the euphoria settled down. The whole team sat around in a semicircle, just listening. And fidgeting. The game was close. The Tigers were up, the Angels were up, the Tigers, the Angels.

You knew it would be this way. Even after the final out of our season, the pennant was still dangling just out of our reach.

The Angels were leading 8-5 with one out in the top of the ninth, but Bill Freehan had doubled and Don Wert walked to bring. Bill Rigney, the Angels' manager, was playing a cat-and-mouse game with Mayo Smith of the Tigers. Smith sent up Lenny Green to pinch-hit for pitcher Mickey Lolich, Rigney saw Green, a lefty, and sent in southpaw George Brunet to pitch to him. Then Smith yanked Green from the plate and replaced him with Jim Price, a right-handed batter. Price flied out to left. One out.

Don McAuliffe was up next. Brunet delivered.

"He hits one to Bobby Knoop at second," Harwell's voice said...

"One!!" we screamed, leaning forward.

"...and Fregosi throws to first for two—"

"TWO!!!!" There was an explosion as every Red Sox player, coach, clubhouse guy and batboy jumped for the ceiling. The champagne, which had only been put on ice moments before, now sprayed around the room. Chaos. I ended up standing on a plastic chair in my wet spikes, with Fitzie trying to pull me off before I fell off and missed the World Series with some stupid injury. But we were going. Oh, we were going, because this crazy, Impossible Dream team had done the unthinkable and gone from ninth place and an eternity in the doldrums to win the American League pennant.

I'd done the impossible, myself, hitting .417 in the last 24 games and .543 down the stretch, driving in sixteen runs and hitting five homers in the final 12 games. I'd hit

The crown reads: BABE RUTH CROWN PRESENTED TO CARL YASTRZEMSKI FOR OUTSTANDING BATTING ACHIEVEMENT 1967 MARYLAND PROFESSIONAL BASEBALL PLAYERS ASSOCIATION

more than twice as many home runs as I'd ever hit before, finishing with a higher batting average than I had so far in the majors, and driven in more RBI than I would in my 23-year career, all on the way to winning the Triple Crown. I led in slugging average, too, with .622, and in total bases (360), hits (189) and runs (189).

I asked a sportswriter, "Hey, do I still get the Triple Crown even though I tied with Harmon?" He said yeah, and I allowed myself another swig of champagne.

When the screaming and shouting died down a few decibels, some guys started shouting, "Yaz!!! Say something!! SPEECH!"

I stepped up on a table, holding an empty bottle of champagne, Fitzie grabbing on to my ankles.

I looked out at all the messy, wet hair and smiling faces turned up at me. These were my friends, my comrades, the guys I'd gone to battle with every day of this long climb from also-ran to league champion. We'd joked, we'd argued, we'd batted each other in, we'd bailed each other out of jams in the field. Each one of us had reached down deep; together, we did something no one could ever have expected.

I couldn't come up with anything very eloquent, or funny, or clever. There was too much emotion running through me to do anything but speak right from the heart.

"Thanks for a great year." I looked out at the faces of my teammates. They looked back up at me. "Thanks for not quitting. Thanks for giving me the thrill of my life." **8**

WEARING THE BABE RUTH "SULTAN OF SWAT" CROWN FOR WINNING THE 1967 AMERICAN LEAGUE TRIPLE CROWN

The Boston Red Sox players, managers and trainers pose at Fenway Park in Boston, MA, Sept. 13, 1967. In the back row, from left: Jose Santiago; Gary Bell; Dave Morehead; Jerry Stephenson; Jim Lonborg; Darrell Brandon; Albert "Sparky" Lyle; John Wyatt; Dan Osinski; Lee Stange; and Bill Landis. Middle row, from left: Keith Rosenfield, batboy; Rico Petrocelli; Joe Foy; Mike Andrews; Ken Harrelson; Elston Howard; Mike Ryan; George Thomas; Dalton Jones; Jose Tartabull; Norm Siebern; Jimmy Jackson, bat boy; and equipment managers Vince Orlando and Don Fitzpatrick. Front row, from left: Tony Conigliaro; Carl Yastrzemski; Jerry Adair; Sal Maglie, coach; Bobby Doerr, coach; Dick Williams, manager; Eddie Popowski, coach; Al Lakeman, coach; Reggie Smith; George Scott; Tom Dowd, traveling secretary; and Buddy LeRoux, trainer.

Red Sox
TEAM

Carl Yastrzemski
PLAYER

06
CHAPTER NO.

143

Red Sox
TEAM

Carl Yastrzemski
PLAYER

07
CHAPTER NO.

145

CLOSE BUT NO CIGAR

A Series for the Ages and its Aftermath

October 4, 1967

M y eye picked the ball up a millisecond after the release. A millisecond later, I knew it was my pitch. A fat fastball. The bat came off my shoulder. When the ball was about 22 feet in front of me, I stepped forward an inch with my right foot and began the swing. Using my hips for leverage, I sent all the power in my torso into my wrists, flicking the bat with a slight uppercut into and through the ball, watching it until the very last moment, as if I could see it smush at the instant of impact. *Crrrack!* It rocketed away in a fast, low arc into the right field bullpen as I watched my follow-through. A textbook home run. Now, finally, my timing was perfect. My swing was where I wanted it to be.

Unfortunately, Game 1 of the World Series had ended an hour ago. Bob Gibson had shut us down, pitching a six-hitter in a 2-1 Cardinals win.

Joe Foy picked up another ball behind the screen and went into his windup while Hawk Harrelson and Rico Petrocelli looked on from outside the batting cage. Behind them, a bunch of reporters snapped pictures and scribbled in their notebooks. I guess they'd never seen anyone take BP after a game, least of all in the World Series.

The weather in Boston was awful the day before Game 1, too cold and drizzly to get batting practice in. Then Wednesday, when I most needed a good long BP to get my timing right, tune my swing and shake off the hangover of the pennant race, when we all needed that, someone screwed up the pregame schedule when we showed up at Fenway.

GAME 1 OF THE 1967 WORLD SERIES WAS PROBABLY MY FINEST DAY IN THE FIELD. IN THE FOURTH, I PICKED UP LOU BROCK'S SINGLE CLEANLY AND MADE MY BEST THROW TO HOME TO CATCH JULIAN JAVIER AT THE PLATE.

P

45

30

A

Here, I just reach Curt Flood's line drive in the top of the fifth.

Red Sox
TEAM

Carl Yastrzemski
PLAYER

07
CHAPTER NO.

149

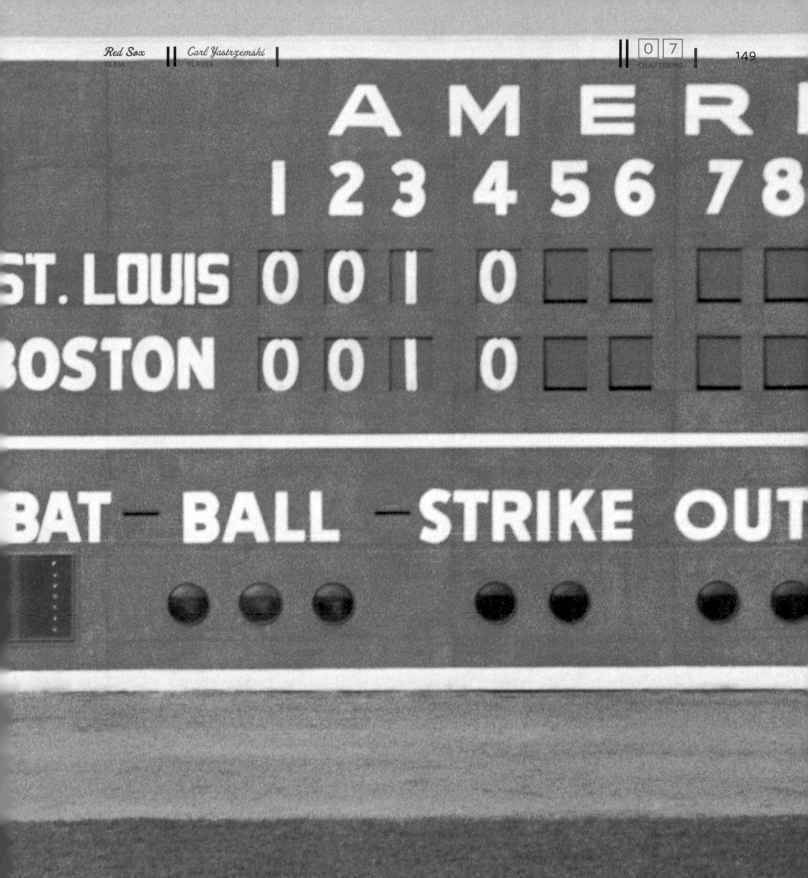

Instead of 45 minutes of BP, we got only 20. After a two-day layoff, it wasn't enough. Not for me, anyway. When the game started, I was still cold and tight.

Bob Gibson was one of the greatest pitchers in the game, in any era. But in that first game, he threw me a couple of pitches I should have hit out of the park—would have, if I'd had my bat going. Instead, I went 0 for four and the only run support Jose Santiago got was a homer he hit himself.

After it was over I had to get loose, had to work the kinks of that game out of my system and get back on that peak performance high. It was a good workout, a great work-out, throwing and hitting for more than an hour. Afterwards I told the club photographer, "I'm going to hit a couple out tomorrow."

Lonborg started Game 2. He was golden, coming one hit shy of a no-hitter. For myself, I hit a couple out in our 5-0 win.

All I got out of the third game, played at Busch Stadium, was a fastball on my calf. The pitcher, Nelson Briles, threw way behind me in retaliation for...something. I went 0 for 3 and we lost 5-2. Whatever it was, Dick Williams wasn't having any. "The St. Louis Cardinals are as bush as the beer company that owns them," he told the press. But bush or Busch, they beat us. Same in Game 4. Gibson didn't need to actually plunk batters. He was intimidating enough just pitching to you. I got a single and a double, but it was a jewel of a shutout. We were now down 3 games to 1 and faced the end in St. Louis for game 5.

The Cardinals were a good club, but they were cocky—and snooty. They talked about us like we didn't belong. The Red Sox wives were given third-class treatment in the hospitality suite. The Cards didn't even bother bringing their luggage to the park for Game 5. They were convinced they were going to wrap it up at home.

But they obviously didn't know Dick Williams's Red Sox. This was a team that had come from a ninth-place finish and 100-1 odds to win the AL pennant. And just to make sure we played with passion, he tacked an article by *LA Times* columnist Jim Murray to the board. "DEAD SOX," it read.

Well, Jim Lonborg didn't get the memo, as they say. He three-hit St. Louis, and before they knew it, they—and we—were all on our way back to Boston for Game 6. We put on our best Beantown welcome by beating up on the Redbirds. Rico, Reggie and I all hit home runs in the fourth inning, on our way to a one-sided 8-4 win.

Red Sox
TEAM

Carl Yastrzemski
PLAYER

07
CHAPTER NO.

151

(TOP) A THREE-RUN HOMER IN GAME 2 IN THE SEVENTH INNING
(BOTTOM) THE SCOREBOARD TELLS THE WHOLE STORY ABOUT JIM LONBORG'S MASTERY IN GAME TWO

It all came down, as in our hearts we always knew it had to, to Game 7. Williams decided to start Lonborg on only two days' rest. Lonnie, like most pitchers, needed three. But we needed a win, and Jim was our stopper.

I could see right away that Lonborg didn't have his best stuff. He wasn't keeping the ball low, and by the sixth inning we were down 7-1. In the ninth inning, I led off with a single. Hawk hit into a double play, though, and when Scott struck out, it was all over.

I'd think, what if? What if we'd had a chance to warm up right before Game 1? What if Lonborg hadn't had to face the Twins the Sunday before the Series and had been rested enough to start Game 1? Gibson was one of the greatest, he won 3 out of the 4 for them, but because the Cardinals had finished ten and a half games ahead of the Giants, they could rest their pitching staff for the World Series. But you put a rested Lonborg up against a Gibson, with me, Rico, Reggie, Hawk all warmed up and ready, and there's a good chance Gibson is going to lose another one or maybe even two of those games.

So those are the wouldas. You think about them, and play little situation games with history, but the fact is we had been faced with one of the toughest pitchers we'd seen in 1967, and the Cardinals were world champions. It was a disappointing Series for us, but it was also heartening to come back from 3-1 and make a Game 7.

And win or lose, the Series could never take away the Impossible Dream, the Miracle of Fenway. It was the closest, most exciting, wildest pennant race I think baseball has ever seen—and we were one of its most unlikely winners. Even now, 40 years later, the Dream lives on in the memories of all the New Englanders who lived through it, and in the Red Sox legend that inspired those who came after.

I got a few souvenirs of that season. The big one: the AL Most Valuable Player trophy. But also Pro Athlete of the Year, the Gold Glove Award, *Sports Illustrated* Sportsman of the Year, the Associated Press Male Athlete of the Year and other regional press awards like the Ty Cobb Award in Atlanta and the Sultan of Swat award in Baltimore. And Jim Lonborg won the Cy Young Award for his clutch 22-9 season.

During the raucous locker-room celebration when we won the pennant, Dick O'Connell quietly mentioned that I'd be getting a $100,000 salary the next year, which, in 1967 baseball salary terms, was huge.

I also got a Triple Crown trophy. There isn't a physical Triple Crown, really—it's just a citation—but the Seagram's company had a special one made for me. It was an im-

Red Sox
TEAM

Carl Yastrzemski
PLAYER

0 7
CHAPTER NO.

153

pressive trophy, very lavish.

There was only one problem: they misspelled my name. YASTREMSKI.

The only team I ever played for was the Red Sox, so maybe I'm not the world's foremost expert. But I'm going to go ahead and say that no city has a relationship with its team like Boston and the Red Sox. There are some special bonds, sure, like New York and the Yankees, or Green Bay and Dallas with their football teams.

But the Boston/Sox relationship—at least up until the 2004 world champion team—has been about fighting back and never losing sight of the dream. The Red Sox mystique is about hope.

That's something people can relate to. You do the best you can, you get close to your goal, but a lot of the time the chips just don't fall your way.

Maybe that's why Red Sox fans, even if they can't make it to Fenway, even if they live in Maine, or California, are so passionate about their team. Rooting for the Red Sox is like life and death, someone wrote, only more serious. And the whole thing gets pumped up by Fenway, too. It's small, it's ancient and the Wall lords over the whole thing. People love it.

The Sox had had some legendary players and great teams In the years after the Bambino was sold to the Yankees in 1919. The "Curse of the Bambino" hit the great Jimmie Foxx's teams of the '30s, and then the pennant-winning 1946 club of Ted Williams and Bobby Doerr. They couldn't get past the Cardinals, either.

As that team broke up and Williams aged, the Red Sox were less and less of a baseball power. By the late '50s and early '60s, when I came along, they'd gotten downright mediocre and had pretty much lost their spirit. But not the fans. True, fewer fans came to the park after "Teddy Ballgame" retired; the early '60s were a low point in attendance in the "modern" era. But even the smallest crowds (which got a lot bigger after '67) were passionate. They cared so much it could be tough on players. Fenway fans would rip right into you. Go into a slump, strike out in a clutch situation or boot a grounder and whew, you'd hear about it.

"You suck, Yaz!"

"Bring Williams back to left!"

And my all-time favorite: "Yaz, you can't even spell your name!"

But then you'd do something flashy, hit a home run or grab one off the Wall and nail a guy at second, and they'd cheer for you that much louder.

Same for the team. I don't know why, after so many years of not making it, but Fenway fans expected the best. So they'd let us all know when we weren't cutting it.

We heard from them in 1968.

Just as it seemed like destiny had guided us to the pennant, with everyone playing almost beyond their limits and the breaks falling our way, destiny then left us in the lurch once we got to the Series. And after the Series, she moved out of state.

I'd been looking forward to the next season, of course. We all had. We had accomplished so much, taking our ninth-place, 100-1 underdog club to within nine innings of the World Championship. We showed everyone that we were truly a great team. And we were young and could be even better in 1968.

The first sign of trouble was when Jim Lonborg tore up his left knee skiing at Lake Tahoe in the winter of '67.

After that, the injuries snowballed. Mike Andrews was out for several weeks with an injury. Jose Santiago's elbow popped while he was warming up after a rain delay. His career was pretty much over. Lonnie could only go 6-10 with a 4.29 ERA when he came back in June. Tony C. had to sit out the entire season.

Personally, I took the batting title again in '68. I got it by batting .301. My average wasn't really even that high—it was .3005, the lowest for any batting champion ever. But that was the "Year of the Pitcher" right there. Denny McLain won 31 games in 1968. Bob Gibson had a practically nonexistent 1.12 ERA, and the average BA around the league was .231. After '68, in fact, they lowered the pitcher's mound from 15 feet to 10 feet, which I thought was a bad idea. It brought in a bunch of tricky sinker ball specialists. I'd rather have faced the power pitchers, the Bob Gibsons. That was my game.

The Red Sox finished 86-76, winning just six fewer than the year before. But now you know how competitive the AL was back then: that put us in fourth place, seventeen games behind the Tigers.

What I worried about more than our finish, though, was the team chemistry. What I was really afraid of was that the clubhouse would start slipping into the kind of going-though-the-motions doldrums that we'd had only a few years before.

And the manager wasn't helping.

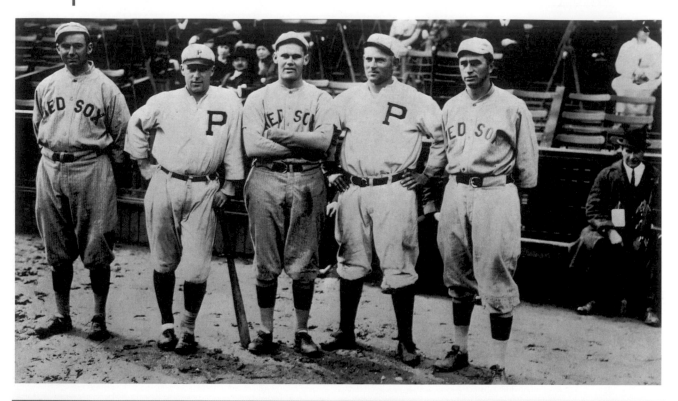

(TOP) THE VICTORIOUS 1915 WORLD SERIES. THE SOX WERE LED BY DUFFY LEWIS, DUTCH LEONARD AND HARRY HOOPER.
ED BURNS AND GAVVY CRAVATH OF THE PHILLIES POSE WITH THE VICTORS (BOTTOM) THE JIMMIE FOXX YEARS, WITH
DOMINIC DIMAGGIO ON THE LEFT AND TED WILLIAMS ON THE RIGHT

(TOP) SOME FAMOUS RED SOX FANS (SEN. EDWARD M. KENNEDY, JOSEPH P. KENNEDY SR. AND ROBERT F. KENNEDY)
WATCH GAME 1 OF THE 1967 WORLD SERIES (BOTTOM) OTHER RED SOX FANS ARE NOT QUITE AS COMPOSED

Dick Williams's intensity and his strict focus on winning had been just what we'd needed in 1967. He pushed us and prodded us and in some cases bullied us to perform. Over the long haul, though, you have to learn to get along together. Apparently, Dick didn't agree.

Dick had a doghouse, and it seemed like the same bunch of guys was always in it—guys who had played key roles in our drive to the pennant. Inmates at Walpole Penitentiary had sent Dick a cutout of a doghouse with hooks to hang the names of all us players, which were also included.

Those cons must have understood what it was like to be George Scott. Dick ripped him mercilessly in the press, along with other guys. He'd enforce extra drills and try stupid things like tying Boomer's front leg with a rope to keep him from moving it when he batted—stuff you wouldn't even do to a horse.

I spoke to Williams about it more than once. But he was stubborn. I know he thought he was doing the right thing for a team that had gotten soft or undisciplined. If he hadn't been so hardheaded, though, he might have seen that the harsher he was the worse his guys were doing.

He and I bumped heads—and came this close to throwing punches.

Dick's thing was always that stars shouldn't be treated any different from any other player. He felt that set a good example. I was fine with that. I'd never asked for special treatment. But Dick had a lot of problems with Tom Yawkey (and vice versa) and knew I was Mr. Yawkey's friend and one of his favorite players. So as Tom Yawkey pushed him, Williams pushed me—and in August '69, he pushed me too far.

We were in California playing the A's, who had moved to Oakland. I'd just hurt my ankle in a series with the Angels and wasn't running well. We had other outfielders who were hurt worse, though, so Dick asked me if I could play that night. I told him I could, but that I couldn't run. I taped myself up and went out there. Right away, there was trouble. I was on third, with two outs, when Boomer hit a grounder just to the left of the mound. I took off, hobbling down the line from third as best I could. Pitcher Blue Moon Odom came up with it, saw he had no play at first and threw home. I knew I'd have to get under that

Red Sox
TEAM

Carl Yastrzemski
PLAYER

CHAPTER NO.

159

throw if I was going to make it, but I also knew that if I slid I'd screw up my ankle so bad I'd be out for the season—or longer. I thought about running into the catcher, Phil Roof. I wasn't steady on the ankle, though. Roof had no problem tagging me out at the plate.

Dick started laying into me, yelling that if I couldn't run any faster than that, or slide, he was taking me out of the lineup. I was shocked. I shot back that he knew I had a problem running. He said my problem was more like an inability to run, that he had had no idea I was that slow, and we went back and forth and back and forth.

Finally, Williams shouted, "One more word and that's a $100 fine!"

I got right back in his face: "Hell, make it *$200!*"

"*$200?* How about *$500?* And I'm pulling you out of the game, Yaz! Now siddown!!"

I didn't sit down. I left the dugout and stomped into the clubhouse, steaming mad.

I'm no Lou Gehrig, but I prided myself on playing with injuries. And I couldn't take the way Williams had dressed me down in front of the whole damn team, right in the dugout. Like it or not, guys looked to me as a leader, so that didn't sit well. I was already ticked off at the guy for the way he treated the guys in his doghouse. The more I thought about it all, the madder I got. After the game ended, I was ready to punch the guy right in the chops. I stormed into his office.

"All right, Dick. Let's go. You and me, right now! Come on!!"

He could see I was hot, and that I had a beer in my hand.

"Yaz," Williams said, "we're not doing anything of the sort. Now get out of my office and go cool off."

I threw the beer at the wall. I stood there for a second, glaring at him, then turned around and slammed the door behind me.

I'm glad Dick acted like a manager. Sure, I wanted to knock the guy's block off, but it would've instantly turned his problems into a team meltdown if he'd been stupid enough to take me up on my challenge. Today, Dick and I are friends. We respect each other. Things happen in the heat of battle; we both understand that.

But it was one more sign that Dick's leadership style, as important as it had been in getting us to the pennant, wasn't working for the Sox any longer. Besides his souring relationship with the players, I really think Tom Yawkey wanted to see him leave.

One day Dick stormed into Mr. Yawkey's office and confronted him about a newspaper article where Mr. Yawkey refused to put Williams in the same category as Casey Stengel, Connie Mack and John McGraw. It was a stupid thing to do. A while later, he was gone, with an announcement from Dick O'Connell that there had been "a communications breakdown between Williams and the players."

The night after he was fired I went three for four, with two home runs and four RBI—and the fans booed me. Everybody outside the club thought benching me got Williams fired. The fans liked Dick for piloting the club to its first pennant in 21 years. But there were two whole seasons of negatives between Williams and the front office. It was time for him to go. His destiny was elsewhere. We'd be seeing plenty of him in the other dugout as skipper of the three-time world champion Oakland A's. And as he's reminded me a number of times, it got me out of paying that $500 fine.

Eddie Popowski took over the rest of the season and led us to a third-place, 87-75 finish. Again, good, but after '67, not nearly good enough. It was the same place we found ourselves in at the end of the 1970 season, too. Third was getting to be the new ninth place for us—seemed like we were stuck there. I was frustrated. I thought we could do better. I thought we still had a good lineup. The problem was that the Orioles had the two Robinsons, Boog Powell and Jim Palmer. They took the pennant three years in a row. So I just played my game.

1970 ended up being one of my best seasons ever. I got the highest average of my career, almost bagging another batting title with .3286. Which I take out to four decimal places because the Angels' Alex Johnson got .3289. I did lead the league in scoring and slugging average, though, and hit a career-second-best 40 homers. I was MVP of the 1970 All-Star game, going four for six with four singles, a double, two walks, a run and an RBI. I also made some nice plays, both in the outfield and at first base, and tied All-Star records for base hits, most walks and most at bats.

Oh, one more thing: over the season I stole a team-high 23 bases, good enough for eleventh in the AL. Not bad for a slow old man.

Take that, Dick Williams. 8

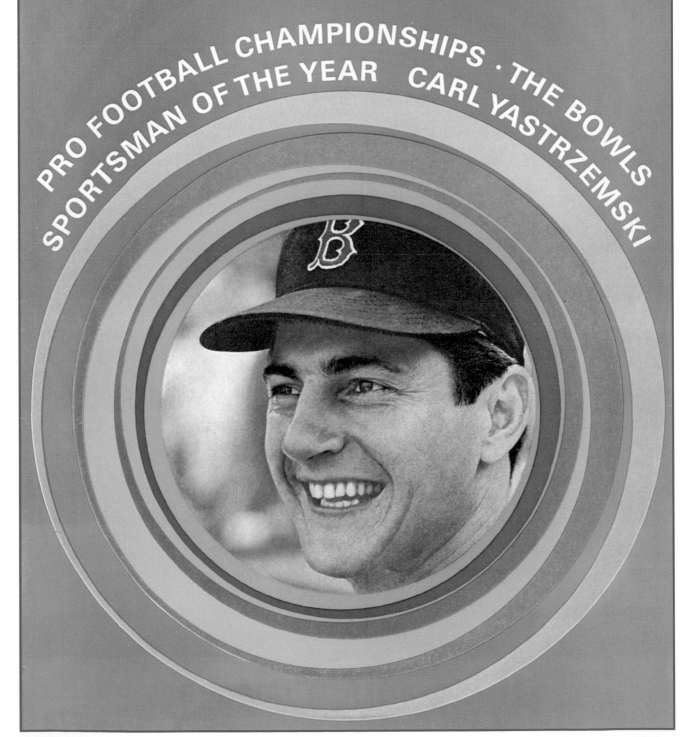

SPECIAL HOLIDAY ISSUE

Sports Illustrated

DECEMBER 25, 1967   40 CENTS

PRO FOOTBALL CHAMPIONSHIPS · THE BOWLS
SPORTSMAN OF THE YEAR   CARL YASTRZEMSKI

YANKEES AND REDS

The Classic Games of a Generation

October 2, 1972, Tiger Stadium

Y our pulse gets faster when you start smelling a pennant. Your eyes are open wider, the colors are brighter, you're taking in everything on the whole field at once. There's a feeling of it on your skin, in the way you breathe. Standing in against Mickey Lolich in the third with one out, I was alive in the way I could only be when we were close to winning it all.

Have you ever tried a Rubik's Cube? Winning seasons are like that. It seems impossible to figure out the right formula, and then—click—things just line up. I'd been out for a month with a bad knee. It took me a while to feel comfortable on it; I'd hit two home runs all year. Then in September—my time of year—I hit ten. And batted .350. We picked Luis Tiant up from a Braves farm team, his career all but over. Now, in '72, he was huge. The closer we got to the pennant, the better he pitched. We had a rookie catcher with an unrookielike .293 average and 22 home runs. We called him Pudge, although his name was really Carlton. And Luis Aparicio, the great shortstop who earlier in his career had led the league in stolen bases an incredible nine seasons in a row, was on a tear at the plate after coming back from a broken finger in August.

The Red Sox had gone from fifth place seven and a half games out when I was on the disabled list to fourth place and four out in early August. Then, later that month, we were in third place and three out…and then second and one and a half out in September.

Now, in October, we were in first place, leading the Tigers by half a game. We had begun our road trip in Baltimore, where I hit two homers and four RBIs in the first two games to give us a nice, fat one-and-a-half-game lead. But losing to the Orioles on getaway day had pushed us out on the edge. As we faced the Tigers with just two games and seven innings left to the season, the pennant rode on every pitch, every hit, every base.

Just the way I like it.

The Tigers were in the same spot. All 51,518 people in Tiger Stadium were hanging on each strike and ball Lolich threw. The stands sparkled with flashbulbs. The roar was like an airport runway.

Detroit was leading, 1-0. Tommy Harper was on second, Aparicio on first. Lolich, the Tigers' motorcycle-riding ace, was sharp. He would fan fifteen Red Sox that day. But I was hot, too. I was starting to feel kind of like I'd felt in '67—almost as if I could dictate games. And this was a place where I could do some damage.

When you're cold, when you're slumping, pitchers can worry you. You just hope to survive the at bat, sometimes. But when you're really on, a pitcher is just a guy standing out there between you and a home run.

And there it was. *Yes! Now!* I took the bat off my shoulder, moved my left foot, ripped the bat across the ball and got all of it. Mickey Stanley was playing a bit shallower than he should have been and moved too slow. As I dropped the bat and took off, I saw the

ball sailing over his head in center. But when it fell short, bouncing near the wall with Stanley trying to run it down, I put my head down and headed into a dead sprint. I could do it—an inside-the-park homer! Or, at the very least, a two-run triple. Harper and Aparicio were off and running. Harper scored easily. I swept through second, leaning into the run, going for third. It was only when I was coming into the base that I looked up and saw the last thing I expected—or wanted: Luis Aparicio, picking himself up from the ground. He had fallen down two steps from third, and now he was scrambling back to the same base I was headed for.

(ABOVE) A ROOKIE TO RECKON WITH, CARLTON "PUDGE" FISK
(OPPOSITE) DETROIT'S MICKEY LOLICH

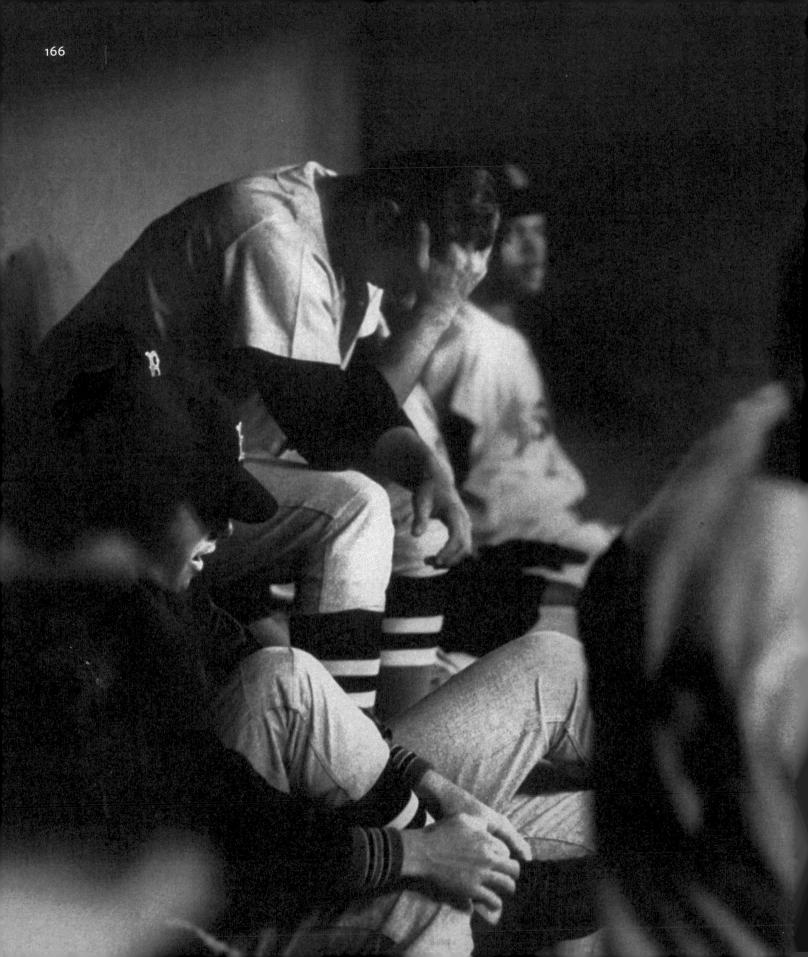

Shock, horror, panic.

"Luis! No!! Turn around! Go HOME!!!" I pushed him away. Aparicio was as panicked as I was. He turned and headed for home again but stumbled and fell a second time. Suddenly his famous fleet feet were lead.

Aparicio could have made it, would have scored even then, but he'd given up on home, he just wanted to stay alive. So he lunged for third. Where I was. I had no choice but to turn around and run away from the base, going backwards, maybe taking the whole damn season with me.

I knew I'd never make it. Sure enough, Stanley's throw came in, cut off by the shortstop, Brinkman, and as the roar from the crowd shook the stadium he and Rodriguez caught me in a rundown.

That was as close as we would get that day—and that year. Lolich threw a complete game, Rodriguez got a home run and three RBI and we lost 4-1. We were a half game behind the Tigers.

The next night we sent out our best pitcher, Tiant, who had a respectable seven-hit six-plus innings. Unfortunately, the two runs he earned snuffed out our last hope. There was a third Tiger run, too, just to put our season on ice, and that one popped out of my glove. I was playing first when Cash, their first baseman, hit a chopper between first and the mound. I charged it, trying to nail Kaline at the plate and keep us close, but I didn't get my glove fully on it. It squirted out before I could make the throw. I threw my head back in one of those awful *if I could only have that moment back!!* moments.

Yeah, we would have lost anyway. We only got one run to their three. But for our chances at capturing the division to end that way, out of my glove, was more than I could take. I went into the locker room after it was over and stuck my head in my locker.

Tiant was inside his locker, and so was Carlton Fisk, who had gotten so close in his first season only to see it slip away in the last couple games.

It wasn't the first time I'd been emotional after a game, but it was the hardest loss I'd ever taken.

We beat Detroit the next day in the last game of the season, but we were already out of it.

Aparicio's stumble was just more fodder for future Curse nuts. The story went that Babe Ruth put a curse on the Red Sox when he was sold to the Yankees in 1919. The Sox hadn't won a Series since 1918 (until 2004, of course). Whereas the Yankees had won 26. I don't see why the Babe would curse the Sox—hell, things worked out pretty well for him.

Although I admit, the Aparicio thing was a little strange. And yes, sometimes funny stuff happened to the Red Sox.

But if anyone had told me about a curse, I'd have pushed them over in the direction of one of our pitchers, Bill "Spaceman" Lee. I'd figure they had lots to talk about.

Look, baseball's a very, very hard game. It's easy to make mistakes. To win, you have to work hard at it. So I worked—always—on getting my hitting right, and fielding my position. I also always wanted the best team we could get, with great competitors who could contribute and help create a good, winning clubhouse atmosphere. I know that signing players wasn't my job, but the results mattered a lot to me.

Good as our 1972 team was, it was just the start. Aparicio, Fisk and Tiant were just the core of the best team I was ever going to play on. But what a core. Over the next three years the front office built on that to put together a team that could beat the A's, the Orioles and the Yankees.

The ringmaster of the great Red Sox teams of the '70s, the guy who really kept us going both on the field and off, was "El Tiante"—Luis Tiant. He was one of those larger-than-life guys, and he lit up the clubhouse when he walked in with his Fu Manchu moustache, Cuban

accent and big smile. Luis had made a splash in the late '60s with the Indians, but then he stumbled, got hurt and got kicked around the minors. He was Comeback Player of the Year in 1972, though, going 15-6 with a 1.91 ERA. He won 121 regular-season games from '72–'78, and it gave us all huge confidence when he was out there.

He had the most bizarre windup I've ever seen, corkscrewing his body around so that he was looking at second base almost the whole time and then suddenly, out of nowhere, delivering one of a dozen different pitches he had. Batters hated it. Fenway fans loved it. I don't know how many millions of times we heard them chant-

THE MANY MOVEMENTS OF LUIS TIANT

ing "Loo-ie, Loo-ie!" When I drove home from the ballpark I'd see kids in the streets throwing tennis balls, throwing their heads back and cranking their bodies around just like Luis.

Bill "Spaceman" Lee, our loopy southpaw, was a guy I was never exactly on the same wavelength with. But I don't think anyone was. He had his own special wavelength. Lee didn't have a lot of power—he threw junk balls, strange, slow, finesse pitches—but all the same he was reliable and very consistent for us until he got hurt in a brawl in '76. He threw seventeen-win seasons in '73, '74 and '75. The secret about Lee was that for all his flaky image, he actually worked very hard. The thing I liked most about him, though, was that he distracted the press. When he would start talking about pyramids or population control or whales or some damn thing, all of the journalists gathering like vultures around my locker would drift over to his instead. I got to dress in peace and quiet.

Then there was Carlton Fisk. He stuck with the club in '72, but played like he'd been there ten, twenty years. They called him "the Commander" because of the way he took charge of the field. In that first year, in fact, he called me and Reggie Smith out, saying the club needed more leadership from its veterans. I told him I led with my play, I wasn't the motivator type. It wasn't the last time we had words, but I always respected his intensity.

Fisk didn't think much of guys who took the game less seriously than he did. And he hated the Yankees. He particularly hated their catcher, Thurman Munson. Munson hated him right back. They were cut from the same cloth.

In a game in August 1973, when we were tied for first, Munson broke for the plate on a missed squeeze bunt, slamming into Fisk like a truck.

Pudge held on to the ball, but Munson tried to pin him to the ground so that Felipe Alou could take extra bases. Fisk kicked Munson off and took a swing at him. Gene Michael, the Yankee batter, grabbed Fisk, so Pudge threw Michael down with his left arm, sticking it right across Michael's throat so he couldn't breathe, and punched Munson's face underneath the pile with the other arm. 60 guys on both sides poured out of the dugouts and bullpens in a brawl that took ten minutes to stop.

Well, like I say, he was intense.

Jim Rice, Fred Lynn and Dwight "Dewey" Evans formed the best all-around outfield we had while I was there.

Rice was a solid 6'2" 200-pounder with all the makings of the fearsome slugger he became. He would eventually take over left field from me, only the second guy to play next to the Wall after Ted Williams. Did a pretty good job with those "dekes," too. Lynn was a natural, a great center fielder, a lefty who hit with power and made it look easy. It wasn't that I was jealous of him…I just couldn't understand it. Here I was, working my tail off in the batting cage every day for almost 20 damn years, and he'd do stuff like hit three homers and bat in ten runs against the Tigers in his first year in the majors, all with these effortless flicks of the bat.

During the years we were assembling this great lineup, something else was happening, something I hadn't felt in a few years: the clubhouse was becoming fun again. Our 1967 Impossible Dream team had been really close…we'd joke and talk and yell and play our share of pranks. But after the club changed and we went from AL champs to third-place also-rans, the atmosphere changed. It wasn't like 1962, but there wasn't a lot of spirit or closeness, nothing to take guys out of themselves after a bad outing and get them up for the next day.

With the arrival of Tiant, that started to change right away.

It was impossible to feel down around the guy. If you were thrown out on a broken bat single, he'd grab all the pieces and tape them together while you were off in the corner, steaming. After a while, he'd come up, roll that big cigar around in his mouth and hand the bat back to you.

"Jew wanna use dees bat again?"

He didn't take anything seriously. If he got knocked out of a game, he'd sit there and stew for ten minutes, then say, "I'll get those sons of beeches next time!" Then he'd jump up and go see if he could cut up some of Aparicio's clothes.

I don't know when the first prank started. A hotfoot or cut necktie somewhere in 1971. But it didn't take long for the pranks to start escalating. Cut ties became legs cut off pants, or arms ripped off sweaters, or whole suits sliced to ribbons. If someone was sleeping in the clubhouse, there was a good chance his nap was going to end with a bucket of cold water. Tiant was sitting on the john one morning yelling out insults to Tommy Harper like he always did, not suspecting that at that very moment Tommy was perched above the stall, tipping a bucket of crushed ice on him.

I'M DOING MY BEST TO COOL OFF THE FISK AND MUNSON LOVE AFFAIR

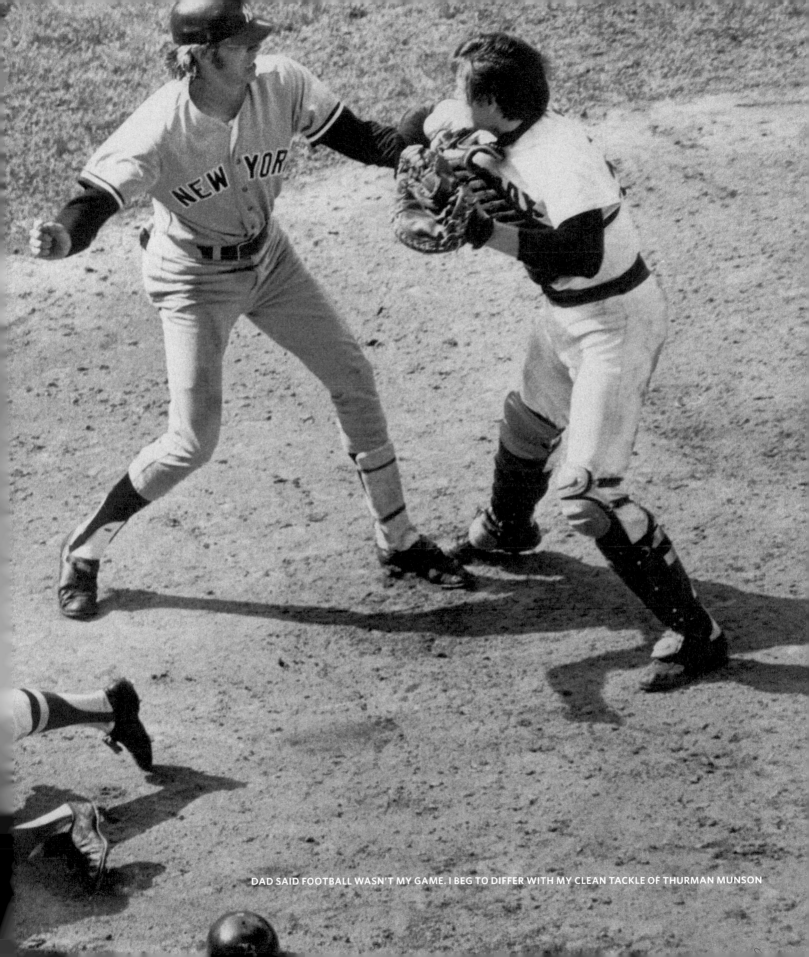

DAD SAID FOOTBALL WASN'T MY GAME. I BEG TO DIFFER WITH MY CLEAN TACKLE OF THURMAN MUNSON

It really wasn't safe for anyone to sit anywhere, in fact. One day I set a fire under second baseman Doug Griffin's chair. Yes, me, old, conservative, no-nonsense Yaz. I confess—I was one of the biggest practical jokers on the club. Inside this focused slugger there was an evil genius who loved making life miserable for his teammates. Like Griff. He just sat there reading the newspaper while the rest of the club stood around watching the fire grow. Pretty soon, flames were lapping around him. Griff kept reading. Suddenly, he shot out of the chair like a rocket. Everyone fell over laughing. You could see the seat glowing red.

Once, on a road trip to Minnesota, I opened up pitcher Gary Peters's suitcase, sliced up his clothes and put them back in. Somehow Peters found out—it wasn't that hard to guess who did it—and set my clothes on fire. Unfortunately, he set my hotel room on fire, too. I got stuck with the bill for the damages. I said I wasn't going to pay. The management was just about to have me arrested when the Red Sox traveling secretary stepped in, wrote a check and shoved me onto the bus.

Because he was such an elegant dresser, Aparicio got it pretty good, and often. One year he tried to sneak back to Venezuela at the end of the season with his clothes intact. He sent his luggage ahead, and was going to leave right after the last game. During his at bats, though, we managed to carefully dissect his traveling suit so that it fell off him the

moment he put it on. I even cut his shoes in half and nailed them to the floor. Luis was going to be met by a government delegation and a brass band in Caracas. He flew there in cutoff jeans and sneakers. And he had to buy the shoes and cutoffs from the Red Sox batboy—at a hugely inflated price.

Bill Lee said I was the worst dresser in organized baseball: "[Yaz] made Inspector Clouseau look like a candidate for Mr. Blackwell's list of best-dressed men.

Guys used to accuse me of having the same London Fog raincoat for my entire career. They threw it in trashcans in ballparks around the American League. I always managed to get it back, though. My fashion choices were very deliberate—I only wore things crappy enough to get cut to shreds.

ONE OF MY FAVORITE SUIT/SHOE COMBINATIONS—POWDER BLUE THREE-PIECE WITH TAN COWBOY BOOTS

Red Sox
TEAM

Carl Yastrzemski
PLAYER

0 8
CHAPTER NO.

175

Then there was the year Don Zimmer and Johnny Pesky got back at me for cutting up their clothes. Pesky managed to give the entire contents of my suitcase away to passengers standing around the Logan luggage carousel—"Here's a Yaz souvenir, everyone!"—while Zim sent me an express, special delivery, COD package. A big, heavy thing. It cost me $148 to find out that the box contained dead fish, dirt and rocks.

When it came game time, though, we were ready. The pranks and jokes kept us loose, and made us want to come to the park even when things weren't going well.

With a great team up and down the lineup, and the best team chemistry you could get out of a bunch of razor blades and matches, my main question was when—not if—we'd put it all together and get to the Series. But as I advanced into my midthirties, I was also asking questions about my role.

After a 1973 season in which we went 89-73 and finished in second place but still couldn't get near the Orioles, Kasko was kicked upstairs to the front office. Under new manager Darrell Johnson, 1974 started out in a promising way. The Red Sox were in first place from July all the way to early September. Then, like a house of cards, we collapsed. The pitching was OK, but that doesn't help you much if you're not scoring runs. We dropped 20 out of our last 32 games and finished second to the Orioles again.

We went into the 1975 season reinforced with Lynn and Rice. To make room for Rice, I took over first base full-time, only occasionally playing in left field for the rest of my career. I was turning 36 and going into my fifteenth season. It seemed like it was time. If the Red Sox and I were going to do anything, this was the year.

It was a lot different from 1967, when we came out of the blue—or up from the basement. We hadn't finished lower than third place since then. In fact, the Sox had never been stronger. We didn't underperform, either. On May 24 we pulled into first place, and except for a few days in June, we stayed there. After we took four from five from in New York after the All-Star break, the Yankees never got within eight and a half games of us again.

I wasn't much of a factor after the break, though. In the first game of a July 2 two-night doubleheader in Milwaukee, with Rick Wise throwing a no-hitter for us into the seventh inning, the Brewers' Don Money hit a grounder between third and short. Rick Burleson lunged and backhanded it, but his off-balance throw to me at first came in high and I was pulled off the bag as I jumped for it. As I came down and tried to make a sweep tag on Money, he banged into me and I pulled the ligaments in my shoulder. The next day,

I could barely move it. I got back into the lineup, but something was wrong. I'd been batting .313 before the All-Star break. After it, I hit only .212. It was an injury that would affect my slugging for the rest of my career and force me to adjust my stance yet again.

Not hitting well highlighted something that had been happening gradually for some time. Time was passing, and I was getting older.

I felt the twinges in my shoulder. I found myself at first base instead of at the Wall in left. I looked at Rico, moving from short to third. I saw Fred Lynn in center, where Reggie Smith used to be. But Reggie had been traded to the Cardinals in 1974. Lonborg, Tony C., Andrews, they'd all been traded, too, along with Aparicio. Rico and I were the only guys left from the Impossible Dream season. We were the old guard.

The younger guys on the club looked to Carlton Fisk for leadership and to Lynn and Rice for the big hits. Along with Rico, I was just helping where I could.

But this was no time to get sentimental. We were still in a pennant race.

Of course, I come from the old school, the age of real pennant races, where you'd play for the league championship in every game, because when the season was over you had either won it or you were an also-ran. Now, in 1975, there were divisional championships, but then league championship series, and then the Series. And these days they've even got wild card teams. Don't get me started.

For now, I just had to keep going as best I was able, do what I could to help the club and rest my shoulder when possible.

In the middle of September, Tigers starting pitcher Vern Ruhle broke Jim Rice's left hand with a tight pitch. Johnson asked me if I could go out to left. I said, without hesitating, "In my sleep." My shoulder hurt and limited my mobility, but Rice was out for the rest of the season. If I could put on a uniform, I was going to be the guy in left.

It felt good to be out there again. Hitting had occupied most of my waking hours since I was twelve, but I took a lot of pride in playing defense. There was more to playing left field at Fenway than just left field. Because so much could happen out there—and did—you never got bored. Johnny Pesky once said I played the Wall like I built it. It's a hell of a compliment. All I can say is that it never took me any time to get used to the Wall again, even on the last day of my career.

The Sox were playing OK ball down the stretch, but not as good as the Orioles. They were playing at a .600 pace, and got within three and a half games of us before they

Red Sox
TEAM

Carl Yastrzemski
PLAYER

08
CHAPTER NO.

179

dropped three out of four to the Yankees in doubleheaders the last weekend of the season. We dropped our two final games, but it was over. We'd done it. We'd won our first divisional championship.

I was happy, but at the same time off-field issues were taking my attention for once. My mom, Hattie, was in the hospital. She'd just had surgery. And, though we didn't know it then, she was fighting cancer.

I visited her as much as my schedule would allow, and Jean Yawkey, Tom's wife, was an angel, coming to see her every day. If you needed proof that the Yawkeys were more like family than owners, that was it right there.

1967 had been a lark, something dizzy and impossible. We were all young, and in

REGGIE JACKSON WATCHES AS WE CELEBRATE THE 1975 PENNANT

some ways we didn't even know what we were doing. I played at a superhuman level. Now, in 1975, the club had new leaders. I was 36, hurt, playing like a mortal and my mom was sick. I'd find out after ALCS that she didn't have long to live. I was looking at life differently. My friend Luis Tiant helped me to keep things in perspective, but still, things had a darker, more serious tone. More than ever, I felt like I had to get to the World Series, and win it.

Once I walked into Fenway Park for Game 1 of the 1975 ALCS against the Oakland A's, everything else slipped away.

Like I said, pennants, championships are...well, they've got magic. They're like a drug. I loved the game, and was lucky to be able to play every day through the season, but get me near a pennant and oh boy, I'd wake up and feel alive in a whole different way. Great players in different sports have talked about this—in football, in hockey, in basketball. It's like there's no time, there are no other worries. There's just the game.

Johnson had sat me down because of my shoulder at the close of the season. But there was no way I wasn't going to be in the lineup for the play-offs, or in left field. If it meant going all the way to Mr. Yawkey, I'd do it. But this was why I'd put in the down years, the hours and hours of batting practice.

This was my time.

Did I play better in the spotlight? Statistics-wise, yes. The Boston Globe ran an analysis of my stretch, play-off, pennant and Series performances and found I batted .417—compared to my career average of .285—with a slugging percentage of .702. For some people, it's all about pressure as you're heading towards a championship. Feeling pressure, handling pressure. But I've never understood that. As I've said many times, pressure, in my book, is when things aren't going well. Like when you're in eighth place, going nowhere, getting booed by the fans and knocked by the press because you aren't Ted Williams. That's pressure. Playing on a first-place club? Playing in a league championship series? Easy street.

And so I stood in at bat against Ken Holtzman in the bottom of the first inning. There would always be problems and worries. But they could wait.

Here, now, in this moment, everything was perfect. I was batting third, starting in left and my mom was at the park.

Red Sox
TEAM

Carl Yastrzemski
PLAYER

0 8
CHAPTER NO.

181

I singled and then barreled around from first on a misplayed grounder from Fisk to put us on the board. Going into the seventh, Tiant had kept a 2-1 lead. He had been bothered that year by back problems, but now he was sniffing that pennant and doing great. His lead was in danger of slipping away, though, when he put two runners aboard. Billy Williams, the A's designated hitter, was at the plate. Williams was a guy who was either going to strike out or go long. He went long. The drive to deep left was arcing away from me towards the Wall.

Even though I hadn't been playing left much, the number of steps to the Wall was as automatic for me as the number of steps to the front door. I ran, keeping my eye on the ball, and just when I knew I'd taken enough steps to be at the Wall, I jumped, hauled it in and preserved the lead.

That was as close as Oakland would get, and we loaded on five runs in the seventh to make it a 7-1 game. We knew Oakland had more than that, though—they'd won the World Series three years in a row, after all. Maybe they didn't have Catfish Hunter—one of the first big free agents, now off to the Yankees—but they still had Reggie Jackson, Vida Blue, Rollie Fingers, Sal Bando and Campy Campaneris.

In the second game, after Campaneris walked, I played the carom on a long fly, threw to Rico and nailed him at third.

I was having a great time out in left. I wanted more. With each batter, I was yelling inside, "Hit it to ME!"

But I wasn't so confident at the plate. Because of my shoulder, I had to rethink my stance. I just couldn't hold the bat high like Musial anymore—I didn't have the strength or mobility, and it hurt too damn much. So what I'd been working on with Popowski and Johnson was holding the bat lower between pitches. I'd raise it higher at the windup, and by the time the pitcher delivered, I'd have the bat where I needed it. I hated it. It was uncomfortable, it was distracting. But it was also the only thing to do. The question was, would it work?

Vida Blue, with his 22 wins that season, had gotten me to ground out to short in the first inning. In the fourth, I tried again. As he wound up with that high, high kick, I took a breath and raised the bat, feeling my shoulder burn. The timing of my swing that had become so unconscious over the years—now I had to think hard every millisecond as I got ready to come out of my stance. Just as Vida released his fastball I got the bat into

position and—Crack—smacked the ball over the fence in left center. It was one of the least comfortable homers I'd ever hit. But one of the most satisfying.

I was going to be a part of this postseason.

We went on to win the second game, 6-3, and headed to Oakland. If anybody doubted I could handle the outfield there, I put those doubts to rest when I took off into the Coliseum's deep left, grabbed a ball Reggie Jackson sent zooming along the foul line

COME ON, INTERFERENCE, RIGHT?

and fired it to Denny Doyle at second to get him for the third out.

"You don't do things like that on me, Reggie," I said when I ran by on my way to the dugout. You know, I don't think he appreciated me saying that. But I wasn't through with him. In the eighth I flew after another blistering liner he hit to left center, extending my shoulder and my whole body beyond where it should have gone even before the injury. I nabbed the ball and skidded on my stomach about five yards, getting up and throwing to Doyle to hold Jackson to a single instead of an RBI triple. The inning ended with Reggie still standing on first. The game ended with me going two for four...and the Red Sox winning their second pennant in eight years.

Because we won on the road, our celebration was a little more low-key than it had been in '67. Mr. Yawkey allowed himself a little champagne. It wasn't something he drank much of.

We actually weren't all that surprised to sweep Oakland. After all, we'd had a chance to scout them when we played in the regular season and knew we matched up well.

The National League champion Reds were a different story. For one thing, they had won more games than any other team in the majors. For another, even though we had scouting reports on them, we hadn't seen them ourselves since spring training in Florida. And even then you're not getting the best idea of what pitchers are going to look like in October.

What we knew about the Reds right off was that they were the Big Red Machine, hard-hitting and hard-running. Alongside their name-brand stars, Rose, Morgan, Bench and Perez, they were also adding some younger guys like Ken Griffey Sr., Davey Concepcion and George Foster. On the other hand, we'd shown the A's and everybody else what we were made of. We had Lynn, we had Tiant, and Spaceman's junk, and Cooper, Carbo, Evans...and me.

The Series opened at Fenway with a five-hit shutout by Luis. I helped him preserve it with a diving catch of a Dave Concepcion fly with a runner on. The next day, Sunday, Bill Lee carried a 2-1, four-hit game into the ninth and then, when he gave up a double to Bench, got replaced with Dick Drago. Drago retired Perez and Foster but then gave up a single to Concepción. Then we got robbed when Burleson's obvious tag on Concepcion was ruled safe. So instead of the game being over, with us leading the Series 2-0, Griffey hit a double, scoring Concepcion, and they went on to take the game.

Cincinnati. Game 3. Robbed again. Reds pinch-hitter Ed Armbrister blatantly interfered with Pudge in the tenth when he tried to throw out Cesar Geronimo at second, but the ump didn't see it that way. Instead of a double play, Fisk overthrew into center and we had nothing. The feeling around the clubhouse was that Darrell Johnson had not

(TOP) WE ALL LEANED FORWARD IN THE DUGOUT, CRANING OUR NECKS AS WE WATCHED ITS ARC AND MUTTERING, "STAY FAIR, STAY FAIR!" FISK LOOKED, TOOK A STEP OR TWO AND THEN STARTED WAVING IT FAIR WITH HIS ARMS AND THEN HIS WHOLE BODY, HOPPING UP AND DOWN, MOVING THE AIR TO THE RIGHT, WILLING IT TO STAY FAIR. (BOTTOM) IT WORKED.

Red Sox
TEAM

Carl Yastrzemski
PLAYER

08
CHAPTER NO.

185

fought that call with everything he had. Bill Lee told all the reporters he'd have bitten the ump's ear off. I can still see Pudge throwing his mask in disgust after Joe Morgan batted Geronimo in for the winning run.

The next two games were decided by the pitchers. Luis didn't really have his best stuff in Game 4, but with some good defensive backup he hung on and I caught Morgan's pop-up to end it in our favor. In Game 5, I singled, hit a sac fly and scored a run, but Don Gullett was, as they say, *en fuego.* The Reds now led the series 3-2 as we headed back to Boston.

> **When anybody thinks about the 1975 World Series, they think about Game 6. A lot of times things in baseball get bigger the farther away you get from them, but when people say Game 6 was the greatest game ever played, I wouldn't argue. And I was there.**

Tiant started because of the rain delay and pitched seven and a third innings, but he got rocked, and when he left in the eighth inning it was 6-3, Reds. We hadn't reached the bottom of the tank, not by a long shot. Bernie Carbo came up with two outs in the bottom of the inning with the score, took Eastwick to a full count and then hit a three-run home run shot to center that brought in Lynn and Petrocelli and tied it up. Bernie stayed in the game in left, and I moved over to first. In the ninth, Doyle walked, I singled, Fisk walked and the bases were loaded. The crowd was making blast-level noise. Doyle, at third, thought third base coach Don Zimmer said "Go, go, go!" after Lynn popped one up behind the base, and took off for home. George Foster's throw was very wide, but Bench hauled it in and set him up in plenty of time. Doyle was out by a mile. What Zim had said was "You can't go—no, no, no!"

The extra innings rolled on with great plays on either side but no runs. When Rose came up in the Reds half of the eleventh, he turned around to Fisk and said, "This is some kind of game, isn't it?"

He was right. It was some kind of game.

Dick Drago hit Rose with a pitch. Pudge's throw forced him at second, though, when he sprang out of his crouch and pounced on Ken Griffey's bunt. The next batter was Morgan, the National League MVP. With Griffey leading off from first, he hit a drive to right that

looked like it was going to land in the seats. But Dwight Evans made one of the greatest catches in Major League Baseball history. He raced backwards and hauled it in over his head, then spun and threw a bullet to me at first. His throw was wide—I had to run into foul territory to get it—but Burleson had been keeping eyes open. He dashed over from short and caught my toss to double off Griffey, and we escaped to the bottom of the inning.

I grounded out to end the eleventh. Geronimo struck out to end the top of the twelfth. It was after midnight and we were starting to fade.

Darcy, the Reds' eighth pitcher of the night, walked onto the mound. Carlton Fisk pulled off his catcher's gear, picked up a bat and strolled back to the plate. On Darcy's second pitch, Pudge lashed out and sent a long and very high fly along the foul line in left.

A gust of Fenway wind caught the ball at the top of its arc and pushed it about fifteen feet into the netting just right of the foul pole. Pudge shook his fists, ran around the bases and stomped on home plate. Finally, dramatically, the game was over. The crowd went absolutely bonkers, and so did the stadium organist. We mobbed Pudge and all hopped around in a big, crazy scrum at the plate.

In 23 years in the majors, that was one of the greatest games I'd ever played in—certainly the greatest World Series game. It was one of those contests where everyone is playing at such a high level that for four hours and one minute—in this case—it's like everyone has been taken someplace else—players, coaches, fans.

If the World Series could have ended right there, it would have been great.

They say that this was the World Series that saved baseball. What with labor troubles that led to the first strike in '72 and the increasing popularity of football, people had been tuning out of the game. Maybe not in Boston, where we packed fans into Fenway, but around the country. However, after Game 6, 75 million people tuned into Game 7.

Things got off to a promising start. I singled in Carbo and Doyle in the third, then scored myself to give Lee a 3-0 lead. He kept the Reds scoreless until the sixth, when, with Rose on first, Lee threw his slow, looping curve he called "the Space Pitch." Yeah, cute. Perez hit it into space, all right—it rocked over the Wall in left and we never saw it again. Lee got a blister throwing those space balls, and he was lifted after Rose drove in a run in the seventh. Willoughby came on with Bench up and the bases loaded and got Bench to pop up with no harm done. In the eighth he retired the Reds in order. In the Reds' half of the ninth, though, with Jim Burton pitching and Griffey on second, Joe Morgan swung on a slider down and away with two strikes, broke his bat and looped a double over Doyle's head at second. Griffey tore home and the Reds went ahead, 4-3.

In the ninth, the Reds sent left-hander Will McEnaney to the mound. He got Beniquez to fly out to right and Montgomery to ground out to short. Two outs.

Two outs in the bottom of the ninth in the seventh game of the World Series.

How many times had I fantasized about this situation when I was a kid? And now, here I was. Walking up from the on-deck circle. Digging in. Touching my helmet, my belt, my shirt, hitching up my pants, touching the tip of the bat to the ground. Shutting out the crowd. Locking my eyes on McEnaney.

This was no time for singles. I wanted to tie it up. I wanted a home run. Now.

McEnaney threw sidearm, a sinker ball specialist. Because the release point is different with a sidearmer, you can swing too early to pull it. *Wait,* I thought...*wait for it...*

I was thinking low sinker ball. It was the pitch McEnaney probably wanted to throw. But he kept it up—and I got under it. Instead of driving the ball, I lifted it. It sailed deep into center...and landed...at the warning track...right in Cesar Geronimo's glove.

And that was the 1975 World Series.

When you lose a Series like that, with games like that, you're depleted. You're physically tired and emotionally empty.

Carlton Fisk said later that the Red Sox won the World Series, three games to four. Hell, we could have won it in five. What if we had gotten fairer calls in Games 2 and 3? What if I had gotten my bat up just a tick in Game 7? All I wanted to do as people filed out of Fenway in gloomy quiet was sit at my locker and run through that last swing again and again and again, somehow making it right. While I took a shower, my mind was still in the batter's box against McEnaney. The hot water ran over me and swirled into the drain as I ran the tapes backwards and forwards in my mind, speeding them up, slowing them down, freezing them, stopping them, wanting more than anything else to have that AB back.

Well, I thought, as I dried off, I had played well. I'd led the club with nine hits and batted .310. I hit .455 in the ALCS. I'd saved some games with my fielding. Fisk always wanted me to speak up more, pat people on the back, kick them in the rear, but when they called me "Captain Carl," that was the kind of performance they were talking about.

Mr. Yawkey moved through the locker room, thanking his players. He stopped by and patted me on the shoulder.

"Next year, Carl," he said.

Yeah, next year.

You know...there's this old story about the guy who pushes a big rock up a hill. For weeks, months, he's shouldering the thing, shoving it, moving it up inch by inch, he gets it up just right there, almost to the very top...he starts to feel the breeze up there...but then the boulder slips and rolls back down the hill again. So he goes down to the bottom and starts pushing again. Eventually he gets to the top—and the same thing happens. And it keeps happening, over and over and over again.

I was beginning to understand that story.

The odds of everything coming together to win a pennant are slim even if you've got the talent. I've got to push myself as hard as I can, play my best baseball, and all my teammates have to, as well. There's a hell of a lot of pushing—and it can always slip away. After that, you've got no choice but to start pushing again.

I sat there in front of my locker, going over it. Well, I thought, guys like Lynn, Rice, Burleson and Fisk were young. Good as they were already, they were only going to get better. Watching them battle a talented Reds team until the last out, playing well in all parts of the game, I knew that we had as good a chance as anyone of coming back and making a run at the Series next year. Maybe Tom Yawkey was right.

I was just going to keep pushing. **8**

PLAY-OFF

October 1, 1978, Fenway Park

The message board flickered on over the center field bleachers in the bottom of the eighth inning.

SOX NEXT HOME GAME TOMORROW 2:30

30,000 fans shook the stands, stomping and roaring. We whooped in the dugout, jumped around and slapped each other on the back.

"It's a play-off!!!"

A moment later the board flashed again:

THANK YOU RICK WAITS

We laughed. There was cheering from the stands. Some of us players were happy, some were relieved, all were smiling and talking at once.

I looked up at the message and thought about everything that had happened since the board was installed in 1976. We'd packed more drama into those two and a half years than ten seasons of *All My Children*. And all of it led up to this point. The season—and maybe any hope of me ever getting to the World Series again—hung on the sixth-place Cleveland Indians and their left-handed pitcher.

SECURITY AT FENWAY HAD PROGRESSED SINCE JIM LONBORG'S BIG WIN,
BUT LUIS TIANT STILL GOT PULLED IN AFTER HIS BIG WIN

It wasn't that our 1975 AL champion team was instantly ripped apart by free agency...it was more like being tortured on the rack. It was slow...and painful.

After Curt Flood failed to get rid of the reserve clause, Andy Messersmith and Dave McNally challenged it again. In December of '75, they won. Now major league teams only "owned" players for a year; after that, whenever their contracts ran out they could deal with any team that would give them what they wanted.

A lot of guys have accused me of siding with the owners, against free agency and the union. Well, for one thing, Mr. Yawkey wasn't an owner to me—he was my friend. But being raised on a farm taught me to be very cautious and conservative. And I learned early how important it is to work together as a team if you're going to survive

Of course I can understand why guys would want to cut a good deal for themselves. It's just that the end result wasn't a positive one for the teams, for the game or, I think, for the fans. Take the Red Sox as an example.

1976 was a year when everyone—the players and the owners—was figuring out how this new world of labor relations was going to work. It was also the year of the "super agents," men who understood this new world and knew to negotiate big deals for big stars. Jerry Kapstein, for instance, who represented Fisk, Lynn and Burleson. All three held out during training camp. They eventually came back, but stayed unsigned for half the year. They'd be talking to Kapstein on the phone on the road and in the clubhouse when we were at home. I'm just thankful that cell phones weren't invented yet, or they'd probably have been talking to him in the on-deck circle, too.

It took a while, but those guys all ended up leaving the club while they were still productive. In the meantime, the clubhouse atmosphere, which had been so much fun just a year before, started to get chilly. Guys were worrying about their contracts, whether they were reaching incentives, why they weren't making as much as other guys. There were fewer and fewer pranks and other fun stuff. When Tiant left after the 1980 season, the fun stopped completely. You could hardly call it a baseball club anymore. It was more like a business.

Baseball is a pressure sport. When you're doing great at the plate, say a .333 average, that means you're failing two times out of three. Even the best pitchers are going to get knocked around from time to time, scored on, beaten and yanked off the mound in front of 30,000 people. So, as I said, those pranks, all that goofing off we used to do, did a lot to keep guys loose. It's easier not to worry about pressure situations, or to recover from a bad game. Which means that players—and the team—will perform better.

A good, fun clubhouse atmosphere also helps bond you as a team. You naturally become more aware of situations in the field where you need to work with your teammates to get outs. At bat, you shouldn't be swinging for the fences, thinking about how your own contract is going to look, when the situation calls for you to hit a grounder and move the runner along.

So with basically the same team that won the pennant the year before, leading almost wire to wire along the way, we finished in third place. Fifteen games out. Oh, there were a few great highlights, like my four-for-four, three-home-run game in Detroit, but it was discouraging. We had the people to do so much better.

Darrell Johnson quit halfway through the year. When we were in Kansas City in July, he called me into his office and told me he felt he'd lost control of the team. I tried my best to convince him that didn't make any sense, but he'd made his mind up.

Just goes to show you how quickly things can change in baseball. The man had just won a pennant; now he was gone. He was replaced by Don Zimmer.

Mr. Yawkey passed away on July 9. There were people who said the business with Lynn, Burleson and Fisk helped break his heart. I think that sort of thing sells newspapers and not much else. The man was 73 and had leukemia. But I know what he saw of the free-agent era he didn't like. In fact, he wanted to trade Lynn and Burleson so as not to deal with the whole contract dispute. He took it personally.

Tom Yawkey owned that club without any partners for 44 years and did things the old-fashioned way. He ran the team like a father more than an owner—certainly he was like a father to me. He loved his players, and those of us who really got to know him loved him back.

Probably the best thing you could say about Mr. Yawkey came from the best player he ever had. In Ted Williams's words, "[Tom] had a heart as big as a watermelon. I loved the man from the bottom of my heart. He was unselfish, fair, sincere and honest."

Jean Yawkey, Tom's widow, took over from Tom, but the ownership of the club became a real complicated issue over the next ten or fifteen years. Haywood Sullivan and

Buddy LeRoux, our former trainer, were partners at various points. The tone in the front office really changed. Between more bottom-line-oriented players and a more bottom-line-oriented ownership, I really missed Mr. Yawkey's personal touch. The man cared about baseball first. Money came in a distant second.

We stumbled into 1977. Contract troubles and injuries flared up right from spring training. Our ace, Luis Tiant, held out until the end of camp. Dewey Evans hurt his knee and was on the DL for most of the season. Fred Lynn tore ligaments in his ankle and missed the first five weeks. The Spaceman wasn't the same pitcher after he'd screwed up his shoulder the previous May fighting the Yankees' Graig Nettles.

We still had a strong squad, though. In spite of all the injuries and noise we managed to stay competitive, leading the Yankees for most of the summer. Then, after skidding into a seven-game losing streak in August, we clawed our way back within a game and a half of New York on the eve of a three-game series against them in mid-September. We couldn't close the deal, though. We dropped two out of three and couldn't catch up.

It was a pretty good year for me, though, one that gave me a good reason to look forward to 1978. At 37, when I'd thought my days in the outfield were more or less over, I was put back into left for most games. Dewey's injury forced us to shuffle around the outfield. It ended up being the only season where I didn't make one error. That led all other fielders, as did my 22 assists, and won my seventh Gold Glove. I wasn't too bad at the plate, either, netting a .296 average, hitting 28 homers and driving in 102 runs.

I stole eleven bases, too. Not bad! For me, anyway. OK, so Freddie Patek won the AL title with 53, and Frank Taveras in Pittsburgh got 70. They had younger legs.

Then, in January, my mom passed away. She'd outlived the doctors' expectations by a mile—back in '75, they'd given her six months. She was a tough woman, or I should say strong, because she was also incredibly caring. In a lot of ways she had held the whole extended family together up on Long Island. And since Dad had given up farming and had

(TOP) EVEN MR. YAWKEY KIDDED ME ABOUT MY SARTORIAL CHOICES
(BOTTOM) DON ZIMMER KEPT HIS COOL ALL YEAR

moved to the Boston area in 1967, she'd continued to take care of her brother and sister, who had cancer, too—even while she was battling it herself.

I missed her a lot. She was my biggest fan and my guiding light, always making sure I did the right thing. And the right thing to do here was to dedicate the season to her and help the Sox get one more pennant.

We'd need more pitchers to try, though. The guy who led the club in winds in '77 was Bill Campbell, a relief pitcher (and an expensive free agent acquisition). So we grabbed another free agent, 6'5" Mike Torrez, who'd just won two World Series games with the Yankees, and Dennis Eckersley, who'd win 20 games as a starter that year. To help Campbell, we added to the bullpen.

With these new arms, and with contract problems in the background for the moment, the 1978 season started out in a promising way. By July 19, we'd ridden Torrez and Eck to a fourteen-game lead over the Yankees, who were buried in fourth place behind the

(LEFT) FRED LYNN GIVING IT HIS ALL (RIGHT) BILL "SPACEMAN" LEE

Brewers and Orioles. It wasn't that the Brewers and Orioles didn't matter; we just wanted to put as much distance between us and New York as we could.

Of course, the "Bronx Zoo" looked like it might be doing a good enough job on itself. The Yankees had a 47-42 record. Catfish Hunter and Thurman Munson were on the disabled list. For the second year in a row, manager Billy Martin challenged Reggie Jackson to a fight in the dugout in front of the TV cameras, this time because Jackson ignored Martin's swing sign and bunted. On July 23, Martin said about Jackson and George Steinbrenner, who'd been convicted of campaign finance violations, "They're made for each other. One's a born liar and the other's convicted."

Martin resigned the next day. Steinbrenner replaced Martin with Bob Lemon. About that time, Hunter, Munson and other injured players came off the DL, and they started winning a few games. Still, Reggie said, they were so far back that "unless Boston falls apart, we can't catch them with a motorcycle."

You know, I almost wish we did know about the Curse back then. It would have made it a lot simpler to explain what happened next.

From August 31 to September 16 we lost thirteen out of seventeen. In the same period, the Yankees won fourteen out of seventeen.

Looked like Reggie had gotten his motorcycle.

We'd had our injuries: My wrist had been hit by a pitch earlier in the season and it had never really healed right. My fingers were numb for a while. I couldn't take a full swing and was having to give the bat kind of a flip to compensate for the lack of power and range in my wrist. My back was killing me. Dewey Evans had dizziness and vision problems since getting beaned by Mike Parrott on August 28. Half our infield had bone chips. Third baseman Butch Hobson was making throwing errors almost every day, but Zim wouldn't bench him; he needed Hobson's bat.

Our pitchers were all slumping at the same time. Tiant had a bad August. Almost every other starting pitcher was getting sent to the bullpen. Mike Torrez, who started with a 15-6 record, was slumping. He and Jim Rice were taking potshots at each other. We were tight. We were making errors. We weren't acting, playing or thinking like winners.

The low point was the "Boston Massacre." In four games at Fenway the second weekend in September, the Yankees outscored us 42-9, outhit us 67-30 and swept the series. We went into the weekend four games up on the Yankees. When it was over, we'd completely lost that lead. We kept losing, too—five out of the next six—and made three errors in one inning against the Orioles. We bracketed the week with another three-game series against the Yankees, dropping two.

Very quickly, we found ourselves three and a half out with fourteen games left in the season.

It's not as if we had a big, formal team meeting. It wasn't like that in '78. We were professionals. Most of us had been on our pennant-winning club in 1975. With our backs against the wall, we knew what to do.

We took the last of the set from the Yanks, took two out of three from the Tigers in Detroit, two out of three in Toronto, and kept winning. We were one down on the Yankees. We couldn't afford to lose one more game. Neither could they. Don Zimmer and Bob Lemon were glued to the radio listening to every out of each other's games. It reminded me of old movies of submarine commanders playing cat-and-mouse under the Atlantic.

On Tuesday, September 26, we started a four-game series against Detroit, while the Yankees started three against Toronto. It was around this time that I signed my first multi-year contract with the club. That's right, after almost eighteen seasons with the Red Sox, they figured maybe I'd develop into something. The truth of the matter was that I had always worked one-year contracts on a handshake basis; I figured I'd do better next year and didn't want to lock myself in. At this stage in my career and, by coincidence, at this stage in our season, confidence and security were more important.

"I'm tired of people talking about us choking," I told the press. "Nobody is to blame for what happened to us in the last five weeks. We started the season with 25 guys. 25 will stand up if we win. 25 will stand up if we lose."

DWIGHT (DEWEY) EVANS WAS ALL GAME

Red Sox
TEAM

|| Carl Yastrzemski |
PLAYER

|| 0 9 |
CHAPTER NO.

201

Eck went out there and blanked the Tigers Tuesday. Jim Rice hit his 44th homer. Jim was having a hell of a year, leading the league in almost every category, and was on his way to an MVP title. He was a big reason why we were still in the race. The Yankees kept pace that night. Wednesday it was Luis, who pitched into the twelfth inning to get the 5-2 win. This time he was keeping pace with New York. They'd won earlier.

After catching 151 games, Pudge was battered. He made multiple trips to the mound on creaking knees to coax a 1-0, three-hit performance out of Torrez Thursday night. We'd swept the Tigers. But in New York, Ron Guidry beat the Blue Jays, 3-1. Now it was our turn to host the Jays, while New York welcomed Cleveland. Again, we matched each other game for game. I helped Eckersley seal his 5-1 win Saturday with an RBI double...

...and it all came down to Sunday.

How many times in a man's career can it all come down to the final game on the final day of the season??

The Yankees were still one game up, so the situation was simple: If they beat the Indians Sunday, we were out. If we lost to the Jays, we were out. If they lost and we won, though, we'd be tied at the end of the season. That meant a play-off to see who'd go to the ALCS against the Kansas City Royals.

New York was putting Catfish Hunter up against Rick Waits. Waits was the ace of the Indians' staff, but on a sixth-place team that meant he was 13-15. He wouldn't have a whole lot of run support. The Yankees, on the other hand, were the Yankees, and Catfish was clutch.

Some of us were hopeful about Waits and the Indians; no one was optimistic.

"Do you believe in fate?" a reporter asked me.

I laughed.

"I believe in the Indians scoring more runs than the Yankees."

"Do you believe in Santa Claus, too?"

"There is one, isn't there?" I shot back.

Well, if we weren't completely masters of our own destinies, at least we could do something. We had our own game to play.

Tiant would be going for us, and he was clutch, too. Darrell Johnson had said, "If a man put a gun to my head and said, 'I'm going to pull the trigger if you lose this game,' I'd want Luis Tiant to pitch that game." That's just how I felt.

THE TRADITION OF EXCELLENCE IN LEFT FIELD CONTINUED WITH JIM RICE

Red Sox
TEAM

Carl Yastrzemski
PLAYER

CHAPTER NO.

203

There was no game Luis would rather have pitched than one where the whole season was on the line. When he'd beaten the Jays the week before, he'd said, "If we lose today, it will be over my dead body. They'll have to leave me facedown on the mound."

Nobody was going to have to leave El Tiante anywhere on Sunday, October 1. He was practically unhittable, throwing two hits over nine innings. Rice hit his league-leading 46th home run in the eighth inning, the most by a Red Sock since Jimmie Foxx in 1938, and it seemed pretty unlikely that the Toronto Blue Jays were going to score six runs in the ninth against Luis Tiant. So that was it...we'd won twelve of our last fourteen. Eight straight. In the end, we hadn't fallen apart. We'd stood up as pros, as champs, as men. That alone, whatever happened with the play-off, was something I will always be proud of that team for. We did it in crazy Red Sox style, but we did it.

And then, like a message from on high, that message on the board:

THANK YOU RICK WAITS

Yup. It was play-off time.

A lot of the city had given us up for dead a few weeks ago. Now everybody had Sox fever again. The Cardinal of Boston was in Rome to elect a new Pope after John Paul I died. The only thing he wanted to know before he went into the papal enclave was how the Sox were doing. One morning radio personality Charles Laquidara woke Bostonians up by saying, "Pope dead, Sox alive, details at eleven."

We would have preferred to win the division by fourteen games. But at this point, we were thankful to be in a play-off. And for the sake of pure drama, you couldn't get any better. Red Sox versus Yankees—one game—winner goes to KC—loser goes home. Torrez versus Guidry. Baseball's first big free agent looking to redeem a disappointing season against a homegrown Yankee draft pick and 25-3 Cy Young Award winner.

In the top of the first, Reggie Jackson socked one to left. It had the stuff on it to go out, and with Mickey Rivers on second, they could have broken the game open right from the start. But the Fenway wind that pushed Fisk's ball fair three years ago now blew in from left to keep this one in. I caught it against the Wall for the third out.

There was still no score when I led off the second. Guidry threw me a fastball that I pulled in a curving arc to right. It stayed up, kept curving and curved inside Pesky's Pole

DENNIS ECKERSLEY WAS A PIVOTAL STARTER FOR US.
HE WENT ON TO BECOME THE GREATEST RELIEF MAN IN MLB HISTORY

Red Sox
TEAM

Carl Yastrzemski
PLAYER

0 9
CHAPTER NO.

207

for a homer that put us on the board.

The score stayed at 1-0 until the sixth; then Burleson got a double and Rice singled him home. 2-0. I grounded out. Lynn pulled a curveball to deep right, tight along the foul line. But somehow Piniella was playing Lynn perfectly. He fought the glare, lunged and snagged it to end the inning.

That brought us to the seventh inning. The inning the Sox wish they could have just skipped over.

With one out, Roy White and then Chris Chambliss singled. Lemon sent up Jim Spencer for infielder Brian Doyle. It was probably a smart move—Spencer was more of a long-ball threat, a pull hitter, and the wind in left had changed. It was blowing out. Spencer got it up, but not far enough, and I caught it for the second out.

That brought up Bucky Dent. He was the guy I'd have expected Lemon to pinch-hit for. He was a good defensive shortstop, but a little guy, not much of an offensive threat. He was hitting about .240 for the season—.140 for the last 20 games. And he had all of four home runs.

Lemon and the Yankees were out of infield replacements, though. They'd just used Stanley, and their second baseman, Willie Randolph, was injured.

So it had to be Bucky Dent.

Dent stepped in, probably just hoping to make contact. Mike threw him a strike, then a ball. Dent fouled the third pitch off his foot. He hopped around while the Yankees trainer looked at his foot. Then Mickey Rivers, who was in the on-deck circle, told Dent there was a crack in his bat. The batboy brought him a new one.

All this amounted to a four- or five-minute delay. Torrez played catch with Burleson, but his arm might have been getting cold. Finally, Dent stepped back in the box and swung at the next pitch, a fastball. Torrez said later he'd wanted to throw it tight on Dent, move him off the plate a little, but the delay had messed with his control. It wasn't tight enough. Dent smacked it, hitting it to left, high, very high…but it was playable. It was going to hit the Wall. I was even thinking about my throw to hold White on first as I ran back to the warning track.

But then...that fickle wind.

The ball didn't come down.

With a little puff, the wind carried the ball just into the netting to the right of the foul pole.

Looking up, my knees buckled. I felt like I'd been hit with a two-by-four. I think all of us were shocked. Not shocked that Dent hit it...just that it went out.

You live by the wind, you die by the wind. At times like those I almost thought, what is it that's keeping us from winning these games? Who are we really playing against? The Yankees? *Or something else?*

White, Chambliss and Dent all scored. It was 3-2. Torrez, shaken up, walked Rivers before Zim replaced him with Bob Stanley. Munson got a double off Stanley, scoring Rivers.

In our half of the inning, Lemon replaced Guidry with Goose Gossage when Boomer Scott singled. Gossage got Bailey and Burleson out to end the inning, but we could see he wasn't sharp.

The Yankees made it 5-2 in the eighth, when Reggie led off with a homer to the stands in center.

Because of the pictures of Bucky Dent that are fixed in everyone's memory, I think a lot of people might have forgotten that it only happened in the top of the seventh inning.

Maybe they thought that hit ended it. But there was still a lot of baseball to play. In the bottom of the eighth, Jerry Remy got a double off Gossage and reached home on my single to center, and then I scored on Lynn's single. We were down by just a run, 5-4.

Zim used three pitchers in the ninth, but we held them to a single. Dewey flied out to left. Gossage couldn't get into his groove, though. He walked Burleson. Then Remy hit a liner to Lou Piniella in right field. I could see Piniella had lost the ball in the afternoon light and shadows. But I have to hand it to him. He stayed cool and ran a deke of his own on Burleson. He just stood there, like he could actually see where it was and that it was going to be an easy catch. He froze Burleson between first and second. The third base coach,

Red Sox
TEAM

Carl Yastrzemski
PLAYER

09
CHAPTER NO.

209

Eddie Yost, was yelling at Burleson to run, but Rick was looking toward Piniella in right, not at Yost waving. And he couldn't hear him in the noise. Piniella somehow got the ball on a bounce. Burleson had to settle for second instead of going to third, where he could have scored when Rice flied out to center instead of just moving up a base.

Now we had two outs in the bottom of the ninth and the whole season on the line. The tying run was on third. Remy, with the winning run, was on first. And here I was.

Again.

Goose Gossage was a fastball pitcher, probably the best one playing. He fanned 122 batters in 134 innings that year. Big guy, reminded me a little of Dick Radatz. He pitched heat with a motion that moved his entire 6'3", 220-lb. body toward the plate. You had to know what you were doing when you stood in against him. But the matchup favored me, I felt. I was a fastball hitter. Lived on them, always had.

I bent over, scooped up some dirt, then rubbed it into both hands. A thousand thoughts flashed through my head, a million chess moves.

The last time I'd been in this situation, against McEnaney three years ago, I'd wanted the long ball. I wanted to win it, then and there, with a homer. But with the Yankees holding Remy on at first, that opened up a hole for me between first and second. My best chance, percentagewise, was to place the ball through there—get the tying run home with the base hit, be smart, don't be heroic. But was that *too* smart? Another burst of thoughts buzzed around as I touched the tip of the bat to the ground.

> **OK, even though he doesn't have his best stuff this afternoon, the ball is still pretty lively. Depending on whether it's lower or higher, it's jumping, tailing away or turning in on you just as it comes over the plate. I might not get a good pitch to pull through that hole. Maybe I just ought to hit away, get it out there, use the whole field.**

The first pitch came in, a ball. I decided to look for a low, inside pitch, one I could pull through that hole. The count was in my favor now, so I could be selective. I didn't have to wait long.

His next pitch was at the knees and inside, just where I wanted it. I hadn't counted

REGGIE'S PAYBACK FOR 1975 WAS THE CRUCIAL HOME RUN OF THE GAME

Red Sox
TEAM

Carl Yastrzemski
PLAYER

0 9
CHAPTER NO.

211

on that movement, though. You really couldn't. Just in front of the plate the pitch burst in towards my hands so that I turned on it too late, and, a lot like three years earlier against McEnaney, I got under the ball, lifting it up towards foul territory behind third base. Nettles waved his arms, camped under it and made the catch for the final out.

Guys were crying in the locker room when it was over. What can you say when you lose one like that? Zim was great, though. He took a lot of heat while he was with us, and bumped heads with Bill Lee and a few other players. But after the game, he stood tall.

He stood there in the middle of the clubhouse and said, "Ain't nobody that has to hang their head in this room. What you guys did in winning eight in a row to get to this game was tremendous. What you guys did in going down to the last pitch today was tremendous."

It was like feeling that big rock slip and roll down the hill again.

I had a beer off by myself, staring into space and thinking about that last pitch over and over and over again. Second-guessing Gossage, third-guessing myself. In the end, though, it had been the pitch I wanted—up until the last millisecond—and I had swung on it.

When I faced the reporters, I was dry-eyed and philosophical. The most important thing was to recognize what we'd done, not let guys get down, try to build on this.

"Gossage didn't beat us," I said. "Piniella beat us with those two plays. If he doesn't catch Lynn's ball and if Remy's ball gets past him, we win by five or six runs."

Reporters scribbled, cameras clicked and whirred.

"Look, we came back knowing we couldn't lose even one game, and we didn't. We showed our character then. We showed our character today. That's what I'll remember about this year. We have everything in the world to be proud of. The only thing we don't have is the ring." **8**

Red Sox
TEAM

Carl Yastrzemski
PLAYER

1 0
CHAPTER NO.

213

LATE INNINGS

Aches, Pains, Landmarks and a Last Lap of Fenway

September 12, 1979

M ornings were the worst.

I moved my feet at the end of the bed. I winced, gasping at the pain, and gritted my teeth to keep from yelling. Throwing back the bedcovers, I rolled right onto the floor.

I raised myself to my hands and knees. I crawled slowly into the bathroom, dragging myself straight to the tub and cranking the "hot" knob. When the tub was mostly full, I flicked a switch on the wall.

Whhhooosh. Jets came on and turned the tub into the swirling Jacuzzi that let me stand up each day.

An hour later, when I could put shoes on my feet and walk—sort of—I left the house to drive to the ballpark early. I made my way slowly inside, put on shorts and then shuffled into the training room.

"Hey, Charlie," I said.

"G'morning, Yaz! How ya doin'?"

"Well, I got here. That's something, at least. You got any more tape?"

"I don't know...club's going broke on accounta you, buying this stuff!"

"Yeah, well, take it out of my salary. Now tape me up, Charlie—then carry me out onto the field. There's a game in a few hours, you know. I want to get some BP in."

I sat on the training table. Charlie Moss, our trainer, kneeled down beside me and put a bunch of stuff on the table beside him: elastic tape, white athletic tape, clear tape, scissors, pads, bandages.

He prewrapped my feet and ankles, calves and shins practically up to my thigh. He put in pads so I would not get blisters, stuck anchor strips to my feet and calves, then started putting strips of tape going from my heel up my leg. Finally, he wrapped tape around and around my Achilles tendon to stabilize it. In the end there was so much tape I lost track. Charlie taped all the loose ends tight, poking and prodding to make sure nothing was going to come unraveled.

The whole thing took almost a half hour.

"That oughta hold you, Yaz." He sighed. "Till tomorrow."

I slowly edged myself off the table, testing my weight.

I couldn't feel my feet anymore. At all.

"Uh...you're a miracle worker, Charlie. Thanks."

I padded back to my locker like an old man. Hell, I felt old. I looked old.

I was 40 and my Achilles tendons were shot. But that wasn't it.

Heck, I took care of myself—I was known for being kind of a conditioning fanatic. At the beginning of the season, at 39, I'd felt great. Maybe I wasn't quite as fast on the base paths or out in left field as I used to be, maybe my recovery from night games and road trips wasn't instant anymore, but I was ready to play.

I was looking forward to the season for a personal goal this year: somebody had pointed out that I was coming close to 400 home runs and 3,000 hits.

I'd be the first player in the American League to do it. That meant it was something Babe Ruth, Ted Williams and Ty Cobb had never done. In fact, just three guys—Hank Aaron, Willie Mays and Stan Musial, all in the NL—had achieved it. While I was never driven much by personal stats—what did they mean if you played for an also-ran team?—that would be something special and might really put a stamp on my career.

And if I could do it on a winner—that would be special. I didn't have much hope for that; our pitching looked sort of suspect. But through mid-June, we were never more than two games out of first. Maybe we could do something. Maybe, just maybe, we could take the division this year.

Red Sox
TEAM

Carl Yastrzemski
PLAYER

10
CHAPTER NO.

215

I was on a great pace. Going into a game against the Yankees Saturday, June 30, I was hitting .299 and had fifteen home runs. I had a great game that afternoon, dinging the Yankees for a single, a double and a home run, my 399th.

Oh, the name of the pitcher I knocked around? Luis Tiant.

Luis hadn't been happy with his Red Sox contract, and as soon as he got to be a free agent, he flew the coop. To the Yankees, no less.

I'd sent a grounder up the middle in the sixth inning that Luis speared and tossed to first. It was a freak accident, one that probably shouldn't be surprising if you've swung at baseballs almost 3,000 times, but I pulled my Achilles tendon making that out. It hurt like someone had taken a razor to my foot. I kept playing the rest of the game—getting my home run in the ninth—and I DHed the next day. Maybe because I was favoring one foot now, I blew out the other Achilles later in July.

I hobbled through the rest of the season, literally. I couldn't hit with as much power; I couldn't run. There were times when I could barely walk. But I played as much as I could, mostly as a DH. I always thought showing up and playing was the right thing to do by the fans and other, younger players who might have looked to me for leadership—but now, being so close to that 400/3,000 mark, with such a buzz around it, there was additional pressure for me to make both marks that year.

On July 24, almost a month after number 399, I finally hit number 400 off Oakland's Mike Morgan. The Fenway crowd went nuts, and made me take not one but two curtain calls. I was now eighteenth on the all-time list, which was great, but that 3,000th hit loomed over everything.

It was a strange season. I should have been riding high reaching those landmarks. But the reality was that I was banged up, and feeling pressure like I hadn't felt before. I was slumping, too. 13 for 79. The whole team was starting to slump with me, going from two games to three games to five games to eight games out, and slipping to third place by late July. With the Sox falling out of contention, the fans focused on my chase after my 3,000th hit. That made everything tougher.

The best seasons I had, and particularly the stretches where I outperformed my-

Red Sox
TEAM

Carl Yastrzemski
PLAYER

1 0
CHAPTER NO.

217

self, were all in the cause of the team. Like hitting .619 in the stretch run of '67 or .455 in the 1975 ALCS. Now, though I wanted to make my family happy, and all the fans who were pulling for me, I was basically playing just for me. And that was much tougher.

I thought about all of that on that Wednesday afternoon as I got my uniform on and then took out my shoes. The left one was my usual left spiked baseball shoe. The right one was a sneaker I'd had painted black to match the spikes. I found this setup was the only way I could hit the ball with any kind of power and stay standing up in front of the fans—all without crippling myself.

I thought about mortality. Not about death, so much—I was a little young for that—but about how my body was beginning to tell me I couldn't do it all anymore. And the injuries, aches and pains were adding up after nineteen years in the major leagues. The last year I'd had wrist and knee problems. This year, both Achilles tendons. My shoulders were killing me. Who knew what might be down the road? I always knew there'd be an end to my life in baseball, but it was another thing to start to feel it. And it didn't feel so great.

I thought about Luis. I hated to see him in pinstripes. What really hurt, though, was not seeing him in our clubhouse. I always felt that when we lost Luis to free agency, we lost the heart and soul of our club. He was the only 20-game winner we had. Losing that was a big blow. And almost as important to me was the spirit he added to the club. The sunny, funny, practical-joking looseness that was so valuable in getting a team to bounce back from losses and enjoy playing ball together.

I couldn't help but feel other key guys might follow Luis out the door and into free agency—that we'd lose the core of our last pennant-winning team. And within a year or two, I'd be proven right. I didn't see the talent coming into the club to replace that, either.

All of this took on a sharper edge when I thought about where we were then: twelve and a half games behind the Orioles.

But while I tied my shoes and retied them, trying to get them just right, what my mind came back to was the personal inconveniences the chase after 3,000 was causing me. Geez, I was paying a bunch of money to keep all the out-of-town Yastrzemskis and Skoniecznys in Boston so they could see me hit it. My family and I were living mostly in Florida then, but my kids were spending their time hanging around Fenway rather than going to their school in Florida. Great. They were probably going to be held back a grade and then have all kinds of problems on account of their old man and his stupid record.

Well, there was nothing to do but go out and try to hit the damn thing.

I shuffled out to the batting cage. Walt Hriniak, our batting coach, was at the mound with a bucket of balls. Walt had given me something to think about a few days before.

"You've had almost 3,000 hits, Yaz—and only 400-something of them were home runs. And now you're trying to hit a home run, aren't you?"

I put my head down and kicked at the dirt. "Uh, yeah, I guess I am."

"Well, look," Walt said, "if your 3,000th hit goes out, you're not going to get it back. If you hit it into the stands, some fan will keep it. If you get a base hit, though, they stop the game, and you get it back."

He was right on both counts. If only 13% of my hits had been for home runs, I'd better just try to make contact if I wanted to get 3,000 out of the way.

I always tried to make myself available to the public—I realized they were the ones who were ultimately paying my salary. But I'd be happy when this whole thing was over with. Groups everywhere wanted me to speak to them, resort hotels wanted me to address their guests, everybody wanted autographed balls, there were commemorative hats, T-shirts, buttons, posters, the White House wanted a time when I could speak with President Jimmy Carter after I hit it. It was wonderful...but a bit much.

For three days Fenway had been packed with fans screaming every time I came to the plate, every time I so much as scratched my nose. I had to deliver.

The Yankees were in town that night. Catfish Hunter would be pitching—his last time in Fenway, as he was leaving baseball. How great would it be to get my 3,000th hit off him? What I thought about more, though, was that Catfish had broken into the majors four years after I did, and now he was retiring—something I hadn't even given any thought to.

Catfish walked me in the first and got me out in the third and fourth innings before giving way to Jim Beattie in the fifth. I stood in against Beattie, touching my helmet, tugging my belt, blocking out the 34,000 people who rose from their seats, cheering louder and louder. I hit his first pitch between first and second, a grounder that rolled under second baseman Willie Randolph's glove and on into right field.

Just a plain vanilla single, but fifteen minutes worth of screaming, speeches and trophies. First all my teammates poured out of the dugout and mobbed me. As Reggie Jackson brought me the ball (I made a mental note to thank Walt Hriniak), they set up a microphone near first base. My dad and my son Mike came out on the field, and I was presented with a trophy from the league. Balloons went up. Flashbulbs went off. Air horns sounded. The crowd chanted, "We want Yaz! We want Yaz! We want Yaz!"

Over the PA system, you could hear me sigh.

"I know one thing," I told the fans, "the last hit was the hardest of all 3,000. It took so long because I really enjoyed all these standing ovations you've been giving me the past three days."

I thanked Zim, my teammates and Walt Hriniak.

"Finally," I concluded, "I'd like to remember probably my two biggest boosters—my mother and Mr. Yawkey. They deserve to be here." I choked up; 34,000 people cheered.

The microphone was eventually taken away and the extra people got off the field—me included. Zim put in Jim Dwyer to run for me.

Beyond the 3,000/400 mark, there weren't a lot more highlights to our season. I went into the off-season as a celebrity. I met the Pope, met Elizabeth Taylor, gave President Carter a Red Sox jacket at the White House, went to parties, got awards, trophies, the whole nine yards. It was a huge honor, all of it. In a way, though, all I wanted to do was rest and heal my injuries. One of the things I'd said the day I hit number 3,000 was that I wanted to come back and win another pennant. Tiant may have left, but we still had Lynn and Rice and Fisk, and maybe—with a healthy Yaz in the lineup, too—maybe we had a chance.

But Fred and Jim ended up on the DL for big chunks of the 1980 season. And though I got through most of the season more like my usual, more mobile self, playing 32 games in left, the law of averages finally caught up with me out there after 20 years.

It was August 30. We were playing the A's. I had gotten caught stealing—at least I felt frisky enough to try it—and then come back and hit a home run to center in my second at bat. In the top of the seventh, the A's Jim Essian hit a liner to left center, a real rocket that I was running for, concentrating on the ball—when I lost track of where I was. I miscalculated the number of steps from the warning track to the Wall.

WHAM.

I ran straight into it. I tried to catch my breath...*aagh!* It was like someone jabbed a poker into my side.

220

YAZ
FIRST BASE

AVG. .266
HR 21
RBI 79

TOUCH
COMPUTER
TV
MAGNAVOX

Red Sox
TEAM
‖

Carl Yastrzemski ‖
PLAYER

‖ 1 0 ‖
CHAPTER NO.

221

I tried to shake if off, stay in the game. I hit a single to center in the ninth and scored on a Dewey Evans sacrifice. We won in the tenth on a Jim Rice homer, but I was having trouble breathing. Something wasn't right. I got an X-ray later on: I had cracked my rib.

I couldn't really swing. Except for a few more at bats in three games, my season was over.

That wasn't the only thing that was over: in January '81 the Red Sox front office flubbed and didn't mail contracts to Carlton Fisk or Fred Lynn on time. So they became free agents and jumped ship. The Sox tried to trade Lynn first; there was some legal wrangling about it, but eventually he agreed to be traded to the Angels. Rick Burleson went to the Angels, too. Now, mostly thanks to free agency and contract stuff that came from those super-agents, the guts of our last pennant winner were gone.

Don Zimmer was gone, too. After finishing second, third and fourth, the Red Sox felt they needed to go in a different direction.

On the whole, though, Zim did a good job with what he had: a third-place pitching staff. Now Ralph Houk was coming in, the eighth manager we'd had since I'd been with the club, and he was going to inherit that staff. He would also get a lineup without Fisk, Lynn or Burleson.

Houk had spent many years with the Yankees as a player, championship-winning manager and front-office executive. I respected Houk. One of the best things I can say about him is that he was a real grown up. He treated everyone like an adult and projected confidence. He read guys the riot act when it was necessary, but he didn't do it in front of other players, much less the press. He was a hell of a manager—and probably did better than could have been expected with the kinds of clubs we had then.

It was starting to dawn on me that one of these years I was going to have to retire. I was actually performing at a pretty high level, still—in 1982, for instance, I had my best season since 1979, with 16 homers, 72 RBI and a .275 average. But I was finishing the season more tired than I had before. Travel and playing on short rest were harder and harder on my body. 20-plus years of injuries bothered me over the course of a long season. I didn't complain, but my shoulders, my knees and my heels sure did. I had to change my batting stance yet again, as getting the bat up high, even if I did it slow and late, was out of the question.

GETTING NUMBER 30,00 AGAINST THE YANKEES WAS EXTRA SPECIAL

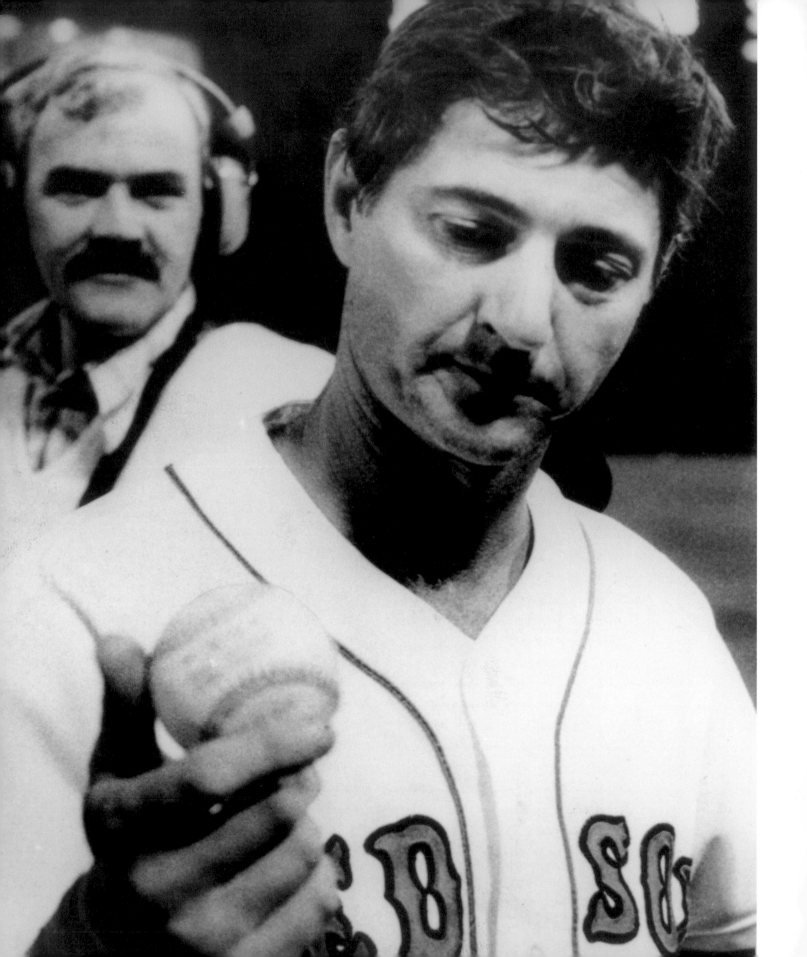

Houk was real good with me, though. He rested me whenever I needed it. He'd talk with me ahead of time about good pitching matchups—and ones I might want to sit out. That made the season a lot easier.

Playing DH helped, too. Over my last three years, I played more DH, less first base and only three games in the outfield. I had always prided myself on my defense. I liked to make as much of a contribution as I could. But the wear and tear of flying back and forth across the country and playing back-to-back night and day games was getting to my over-40 body. The grind of regular defensive play was not the best thing for my longevity—or my productivity in the field. I had to face reality.

More than anything else, what kept me coming back was the hope, however crazy, that I could grab just one more pennant. Yeah, I'd seen Tiant, Fisk, Lynn, Burleson walk away...but maybe another good young team was emerging. After all, who could have seen us coming in '67? Carney Lansford had some pop in his bat—we got him in the Burleson trade and he ended up hitting .301 in 1980—and there was another young infielder who impressed me, a kid named Wade Boggs.

We were good enough to finish third in the division in 1982. And we would have finished higher if our pitching hadn't kept us down again. If there was a curse on the Sox, that was it.

It was starting to dawn on me that we were probably not going to win the pennant in the next year or two. Sure, miracles can happen—some of my teammates were just out of their diapers when I went to my first World Series, so I knew that better then they did. But it really didn't look like it was going to happen anytime soon. And once I figured that out, it tipped the scales.

Getting myself into shape for another season once I was past 40 was getting to be more and more of a grind. Whipping my now 43-year-old body into baseball condition became a big challenge. With my level of conditioning, I think I could have done it more easily, and maybe even have had some really great seasons, if it hadn't been for the injuries. But as it was, the strain of pushing myself to be Yaz every year was making me old, tired and unhappy. You can see the strain when you look at pictures of me in those years. It's written on my face.

It seemed like it might be time to call it a career. I told the Red Sox, and right away word got out and all kinds of celebrations were planned for throughout the league.

DAD AT MY SIDE... IT DOESN'T GET ANY BETTER THAN THAT.

Once the season started, I did what I could to move the team along. Being this odd 43-year-old in a team full of 20-somethings, I realized I had a leadership role that involved more than just "leading by example." I'd not only show up early—which I always did—I'd try to put a spring into my step, too, even when I felt cruddy after a road trip. I'd tap guys on the shoulder: "Let's go now! These are the Yankees—we gotta stop 'em!"

But here's the thing—we started out of the gate hot that year. And so did I. The Red Sox were in first place in early June; I was hitting .323 at the All-Star break.

I was having fun! Why would I retire?

I told Sullivan and Houk I was having second thoughts. I felt bad, not being sure which way I was going, because I knew not only the Red Sox but all the other AL clubs were spending time and money on celebrations and gifts and so forth. But Sully and Ralph were great about it. They said we could pitch all these things as "Yaz Appreciation Days."

Well, our hot season started to cool. Our June swoon turned into a July goodbye as we fell to fourth place, then sixth place. By mid-August, we were twelve and a half games out.

I went in to see Houk.

"Ralph, baseball just doesn't mean that much to me anymore unless we're in a pennant race. It's just not there for me. Do we have a shot at the pennant next year? 'Cause I don't think so."

Houk nodded.

"Yaz," he said, "I've managed and played with some great ones. Get out at the right time if that's how you feel."

He knew what he was talking about.

And my mind was made up...as much as it could be.

I'll level with you; I never enjoyed it.

I never had any fun.

Don't get me wrong; I loved the game, loved the competition.

But I wasn't a Ted Williams or even a Fred Lynn. I didn't have natural size, power or ability like they had. Keeping myself at that level was all hard work, all the time. The thousands of hours of batting practice, before games, after games. The calisthenics. The outfield and infield drills. 25 years of spring training.

I don't know if you can understand how the game gripped me. How after games we lost, or outs I made—all 9,126 of them—I'd be mentally replaying the at bats, in the shower, at my locker, in the car and at home.

And the work, the chase after that perfect swing...it was endless. More than that, it was obsessive. I loved my family, but during my career the game...consumed me. I guess that's the only way to put it. It's like every muscle, every nerve, every cell in my body had one purpose, one mission: to play baseball. It was almost as if I didn't have a choice in the matter. I just had to keep pushing that rock up the hill. It's just...the way...I was.

My former teammate Joe Lahoud said, "We'd be on the road and [Yaz would] call, 'C'mon, we're going to the ballpark.' I'd say, 'Christ, it's only one o'clock. The game's at seven.' He lived, breathed, ate and slept baseball. If he went 0 for four, he couldn't live with it. He could live with himself if he went one for three. He was happy if he went two for four. That's the way the man suffered."

And you know how I knew it was time? When I didn't suffer anymore.

When we lost a game that last season, when I made outs, and I didn't bring that home with me. I'd think about it at the park, then that was it. I was driving home thinking about my retirement, about the farewell celebrations the Sox were planning or about my kids. Like a normal person—rather than Yaz.

Playing for so long, I was something like an institution. A landmark. You'd go to Boston, see the Boston Common, Paul Revere's House and then you'd go to Fenway and see Yaz. For young baseball fans all over the country, maybe even those who'd just graduated from college, I'd been playing their whole lives. Always there, day in and day out. Like your postman or the corner grocer, just trying to do his best.

And when you're an institution, you can't just slip away quietly. First of all, just about every AL ballpark had some kind of tribute to me. I'd asked for no gifts; I got 'em anyway. For a while now, the boos that people naturally aim at good players on other teams had turned to applause instead, like people were appreciating that I was still around. Now that I was leaving, there were ovations and all kinds of wonderful tributes from the fans everywhere I went. There was a two-day celebration planned at Fenway. I wasn't going to fight it—I brought in 123 Yastrzemskis, Skoniecznys and other relatives and friends.

Red Sox
TEAM

Carl Yastrzemski
PLAYER

1 0
CHAPTER NO.

229

Saturday, October 1, 1983. My second-to-last day at Fenway. I started the day out with a big speech. Hey, batting .563 to take my team to the World Series? A piece of cake compared to summing up my career and thanking 30,000 wonderful fans in just the right way.

I barely got through it. I was choking up by the third or fourth word.

"This is a very special day for me. I am extremely honored that so many of you came here to share this day with me. One thing that I've learned over the years is that Red Sox fans are the greatest and most loyal. The spirit at this great ballpark makes it the best place to play baseball in the world. I am proud to have worn only the Red Sox uniform for my entire 23 years. It was a privilege to have worn it longer than any other player. I will miss you. And I will miss my teammates, past and present. The clubhouse people. The batboys. And all the terrific people who work at the park.

I have been blessed with great parents and a wonderful family. And, I was given the ability to play baseball, the finest of all games. There is no other like it. In recent weeks, I have been asked how I would like to be remembered. I hope you will think of me as a winner, because I feel just playing one game at Fenway Park makes me a winner. I loved the competition. I always gave my best. I might not have had the greatest ability in the world, but I got the most out of it.

I don't have any regrets.

Again, thank you. And I hope I represented Boston and New England with class and dignity."

I NEVER LIKED GIVING SPEECHES. THIS ONE WAS THE HARDEST

I asked everyone to join me in a moment of silence for my mom and for Tom Yawkey.

There was a bell that sounded in their memory. As the last bell died away, I said, "New England, I love you!!"

With everyone still standing, I ran around the park and touched as many of the fans as I could. Along the first base line, past right, along the Wall, past all my fans, critics and neighbors there along the foul line in left field and then back past third base. Running along, touching all those outstretched hands, looking at the faces, I knew they could see the tears beginning to well out of my eyes.

I didn't care.

It was all I could do not to grab the mike and tell them I was coming back. How much I'd meant to the fans, how much they'd meant to me...to have that so concentrated in one incredible experience...wow. It was going to be tough to let it go.

I went 0 for four that day against the Indians. But there was still one more game.

"One last time, Charlie."

Charlie Moss taped my wrists with extra care. He muttered something about the money the club was going to save on tape, but I could see he was getting kind of emotional.

Hell, if I'd taped somebody up as much as he'd taped me over the years, I'd be a basket case.

The fans had a sign that day that said, "SAY IT AIN'T SO, YAZ."

"I wish it wasn't," I said.

Then I jogged out to the Wall.

It would be my first time playing left field in two years. I'd gotten to the park early to take outfield practice. Now I gazed up at it, and then at all the fans along the left field foul line. I really wanted to give them a thrill, one last flashy play to give them a great last memory of me.

In the second, Jim Essian, the same guy whose liner I'd chased right into the Wall two years ago, hit a grounder to left. There was a runner on second who took off, rounding third as I charged the grounder and fielded it, one-handed, just like I'd taught myself 24 years before. I brought my glove up, snapped the ball out and was just ready to fire home and nail him at the plate—when I slipped. It had been raining the whole weekend and the grass was pretty wet. My throw was low, and the runner was safe.

Red Sox
TEAM   ‖   *Carl Yastrzemski* |
PLAYER

‖ 1 0 |
CHAPTER NO.

231

I was furious at myself.

I got another chance in the seventh. Toby Harrah lined one against the Wall. As if I'd been playing left every day since it broke my rib, I grabbed the carom, spun, fired to second and held him to a single. The left field fans loved it! It wasn't my greatest move, but they were on their feet, cheering. Getting a standing ovation from my harshest critics in my last game...that really gave me a thrill.

The home plate ump was pretty slack that day, I have to tell you. "If he doesn't swing, it's a ball," he'd told the pitchers. Come to think of it, the pitchers were kind of slack, too.

I jumped on a fat fastball in the third and sent a single into left. The cheers were like thunder. Unless I retired soon, I was going to go deaf hitting singles.

I came up again in the seventh, with a 3-1 lead. This was probably going to be it. Ralph was sending somebody in for me at left.

33,491 people started applauding and didn't stop. I think the announcer said my name, but you couldn't hear it. You would have thought we were in a World Series instead of a meaningless game against the Indians.

YAZ HAT

But meaningless or not, Wade Boggs was on first with two outs. I leaned over, rubbed dirt on my hands and stepped into the batter's box. I dug in my left cleat, adjusted my sleeves, pushed my helmet onto my head, tugged at my belt, touched the tip of the bat to the ground, then raised my hands waist high and locked my eyes hard on the pitcher. Spillner threw three pitches that the umpire decided were balls, and I wasn't going to argue. Then he came over with something hittable. As I began my swing I could see it was a little high. I could have taken it for a ball—and a walk—but that wouldn't have been the right way to go out. In the millisecond as I brought the bat away from my shoulder towards the ball, I thought of Ted Williams. Of what it would be like if I, too, could hit a home run in my last at bat at Fenway. What a perfect way to end a career that would be!

I'll show him I'm a home run hitter, I thought. I'll jerk it out.

But my swing was too low. I got under it and popped up to second.

Oh, well.

And that was it. Finally, I could think, oh, well. I didn't have another at bat with Spillner. Didn't have another game. Didn't have to think about my swing again. I was done. That rock was somebody else's to push up the hill now.

After the game ended, there was a crush of reporters in the clubhouse. I ordered champagne for everybody. I may not have particularly liked dealing with the press over the years, but they were just doing their job, like I was doing mine.

"I'm just a potato farmer from Long Island with some ability," I told them. "I'm not any different than a mechanic, an engineer or the president of a bank."

I had just gone out every day and done my best for the fans. As I hung up my jersey in my locker for the last time, I stood there looking at it and I thought about the cheers, the boos, about all my defenders and detractors out in left. I thought about the day earlier in my career when they were riding me pretty good, just trying to razz me off the field. I ignored them until I took off my cap and pulled cotton out of my ears.

That broke them up.

"We love ya, Yaz!"

You know what? I loved them, too.

I turned around and ran out of the clubhouse in my T-shirt and onto the field one more time to say goodbye. 8

Red Sox
TEAM

Carl Yastrzemski
PLAYER

1 0
CHAPTER NO.

235

COOPERSTOWN

Y he reasons for my election are many. I can never forget, nor will I, the hundreds of hours of help and inspiration given me by so many people. Both In the minor leagues, starting with Eddie Popowsky, Bobby Doerr, Ed Kenney, Gene Mauch, and right up thought the majors, when I started my first manager, Mike Higgins, through my last, Ralph Houk, and also my many teammates who I played with all those 23 years. Starting with the Chuck Schillings, the Frank Malzones, and ending with the Jim Rices, the Dwight Evans and the Bob Stanleys.

I remember in 1961 when I was a scared rookie hitting .220 out after the first three months of my baseball season, doubting my ability, a man was fishing up in New Brunswick. I said, "Can we get ahold of him? I need help. I don't think I can play in the big leagues." He flew into Boston. Worked with me for three days. Helped me mentally. Gave me confidence that I could play in the big leagues. I hit .300 for the rest of the season. I'd like to thank Ted Williams. Ladies and gentlemen, no man is an island. He must have a support system, without which he cannot function.

Take my father. Super athlete himself. Possessing all the talent and dedication needed to make the big leagues, but living at the time of the Depression. He had to suppress his own desires in order that his family could survive and prosper, so he worked and labored toward that end. If ever there's living proof that some people make sacrifices for others, it's my dad. You know, you know, I've often been asked during my career, "How can you stand up to the rigors of big league baseball and its pressure-packed situations?" and I've always answered the same way. Pressure, what pressure? Pressure is what faces millions and millions of fathers and mothers trying to earn a living every day to support a family, to give it comfort, devotion and love. That's what pressure really is, and that's what my dear mother, whom I miss today, and my father gave me, and that's why I specifically mention them today. To acknowledge their heartfelt presence in my life for my accomplishments. I'd like to introduce my dad.

How lucky I am to have been a member of the Boston Red Sox. A truly great organization headed by that wonderful man, Mr. Tom Yawkey. To have played my whole career for one team and in one city, Boston, doesn't happen for many major league ballplayers. The debt of gratitude which I owe him and his dear wife, Jean, who has honored me by being here today, can never be repaid. Mrs. Jean Yawkey, and to you sportswriters who have always treated me fairly and with understanding, you too are part of the support system. I thank you for electing me to the Hall of Fame.

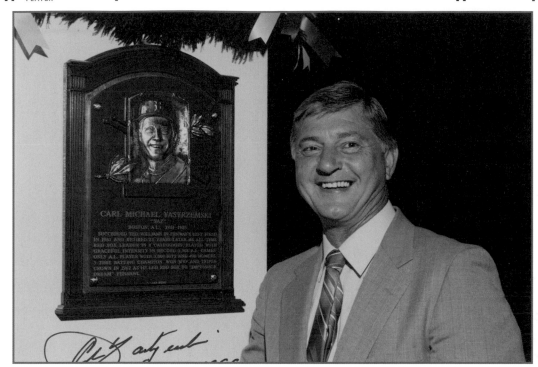

If these are the reasons for my being here in Cooperstown, it's only fair to ask why. Not blessed with the great God-given talent like superb physical strength, I'd have worked twice as hard and twice as long as many of my peers. As the great Grantland Rice said, "And when the one great scorer comes to write against your name, he marks not that you've won or lost but how you played the game."

I can stand here—I can stand before you today and tell you honestly that every day I put on that Red Sox uniform I gave 100% of myself for my own. I treated it with dignity and respect in deference to our fans. A high regard for my teammates, coaches and management. Anything less would not have been worthy of me. Anything more would not have been possible. And if there is any message I can leave on the great day of tradition and honor, let it be this—that the race doesn't always belong to the swift nor the battle to the strong. It belongs rather to those who run the race, who stay the course and who fight the good fight. To those members before me, may you always wear the mantle of your membership with pride. To those of you who are to come after me, may you too enjoy the spirit of tradition and accomplishment that is ours today. You should, for you are like every baseball player who ever wore the uniform of the game. That's why I am so proud today to have played a role, however small, in a game which is America's pastime, and a game which has been a big part of my life.

Thank you very much.

CARL YASTRZEMSKI | MAJOR LEAGUE BASEBALL CAREER STATISTICS

BATTING

Year	Age	Games Played	Batting Average	At Bats	Runs Scored	Hits	2b	3b	Hr	Rbi
1961	21	148	.266	583	71	155	31	6	11	80
1962	22	160	.296	646	99	191	43	6	19	94
1963	23	151	.321	570	91	183	40	3	14	68
1964	24	151	.289	567	77	164	29	9	15	67
1965	25	133	.312	494	78	154	45	3	20	72
1966	26	160	.278	594	81	165	39	2	16	80
1967	27	161	.326	579	112	189	31	4	44	121
1968	28	157	.301	539	90	162	32	2	23	74
1969	29	162	.255	603	96	154	28	2	40	111
1970	30	161	.329	566	125	186	29	0	40	102
1971	31	148	.254	508	75	129	21	2	15	70
1972	32	125	.264	455	70	120	18	2	12	68
1973	33	152	.296	540	82	160	25	4	19	95
1974	34	148	.301	515	93	155	25	2	15	79
1975	35	149	.269	543	91	146	30	1	14	60
1976	36	155	.267	546	71	146	23	2	21	102
1977	37	150	.296	558	99	165	27	3	28	102
1978	38	144	.277	523	70	145	21	2	17	81
1979	39	147	.270	518	69	140	28	1	21	87
1980	40	105	.275	364	49	100	21	1	15	50
1981	41	91	.246	338	36	83	14	1	7	53
1982	42	131	.275	459	53	126	22	1	16	72
1983	43	119	.266	380	38	101	24	0	10	56
		3,308	.285	11,988	1,816	3,419	646	59	452	1,844

MAJOR LEAGUE BASEBALL CAREER STATISTICS

BATTING

Stolen Bases	Caught Stealing	Walks	Strike Outs	On-Base %	Slugging %	Total Bases	Sacrifice Bunts	Sac Flies	Intentional Walks	All Star Selection
6	5	50	96	.324	.396	231	2	5	3	
7	4	66	82	.363	.469	303	2	2	7	
8	5	95	72	.418	.475	271	1	1	6	All Star
6	5	75	90	.374	.451	256	1	1	6	All Star
7	6	70	58	.395	.536	265	2	4	8	All Star
8	9	84	60	.368	.431	256	0	1	10	All Star
10	8	91	69	.418	.622	360	1	5	11	All Star
13	6	119	90	.426	.495	267	0	4	13	All Star
15	7	101	91	.362	.507	306	0	2	9	All Star
23	13	128	66	.452	.592	335	0	2	12	All Star
8	7	106	60	.381	.392	199	0	5	12	All Star
5	4	67	44	.357	.391	178	0	9	3	All Star
9	7	105	58	.407	.463	250	1	6	13	All Star
12	7	104	48	.414	.445	229	0	11	16	All Star
8	4	87	67	.371	.405	220	0	2	12	All Star
5	6	80	67	.357	.432	236	1	8	6	All Star
11	1	73	40	.372	.505	282	0	11	6	All Star
4	5	76	44	.367	.423	221	1	8	8	All Star
3	3	62	46	.346	.450	233	0	8	8	All Star
0	2	44	38	.350	.462	168	1	3	5	
0	1	49	28	.338	.355	120	0	3	4	
0	1	59	50	.358	.431	198	0	3	1	All Star
0	0	54	29	.359	.408	155	0	1	11	All Star
168	**116**	**1,845**	**1,393**	**.379**	**.462**	**5,539**	**13**	**105**	**190**	**19**

POSTSEASON		Games Played	Batting Average	At Bats	Runs Scored	Hits	2B	3B	HR	RBI	Walks	Strike Outs	On-Base %	Slugging %
	WS	7	.400	25	4	10	2	0	3	5	4	1	.500	.840
	ALCS	3	.455	11	4	5	1	0	1	2	1	1	.500	.818
	WS	7	.310	29	7	9	0	0	0	4	4	1	.382	.310

FIELDING

| | | | | | | | | | | Games Played | | | |
Year	Age	Postion	Games Played	Putouts	Assists	Errors	Double Plays	Fielding %		Left Field	Center Field	Right Field	Gold Glove
1961	21	OF	147	248	12	10	1	.963		147	0	0	
1962	22	OF	160	329	15	11	3	.969		160	0	0	
1963	23	OF	151	283	18	6	3	.980		151	1	0	Gold Glove
1964	24	OF	148	372	19	11	3	.973		18	131	0	
		3B	2	0	5	0	1	1.000					
1965	25	OF	130	222	11	3	2	.987		125	7	1	Gold Glove
1966	26	OF	158	310	15	5	2	.985		157	1	0	
1967	27	OF	161	297	13	7	1	.978		161	1	0	Gold Glove
1968	28	OF	155	301	12	3	3	.991		154	1	0	Gold Glove
		1B	3	14	1	0	1	1.000					
1969	29	OF	143	246	17	4	2	.985		140	3	0	Gold Glove
		1B	22	181	21	2	29	.990					
1970	30	1B	94	696	61	8	62	.990					
		OF	69	120	3	6	0	.953		67	3	0	
1971	31	OF	146	281	16	2	4	.993		146	0	0	Gold Glove
1972	32	OF	83	141	10	4	1	.974		83	0	0	
		1B	42	357	33	4	34	.990					
1973	33	1B	107	912	56	6	85	.994					
		3B	31	37	63	12	2	.893					
		OF	14	30	0	0	0	1.000		14	0	0	
1974	34	1B	84	707	44	2	67	.997					
		OF	63	99	2	4	1	.962		63	0	0	
		DH	4	0	0	0	0	N.A.					
1975	35	1B	140	1202	87	5	103	.996					
		OF	8	15	1	0	0	1.000		8	0	0	
		DH	2	0	0	0	0	N.A.					

Year	Age	Postion	Games Played	Putouts	Assists	Errors	Double Plays	Fielding %		Left Field	Center Field	Right Field	Gold Glove
1976	36	1B	94	829	52	2	78	.998					
		OF	51	93	3	2	0	.980		51	0	0	
		DH	10	0	0	0	0	N.A.					
1977	37	OF	140	287	16	0	1	1.000		138	0	2	Gold Glove
		1B	7	57	6	0	4	1.000					
		DH	6	0	0	0	0	N.A.					
1978	38	OF	71	136	8	2	2	.986		63	8	0	
		1B	50	387	41	3	47	.993					
		DH	27	0	0	0	0	N.A.					
1979	39	DH	56	0	0	0	0	N.A.					
		1B	51	466	55	2	42	.996					
		OF	36	63	1	2	0	.970		36	0	0	
1980	40	DH	19	0	0	0	0	N.A.					
		OF	39	65	3	0	1	1.000		34	1	4	
		1B	16	160	10	4	19	.977					
1981	41	DH	48	0	0	0	0	N.A.					
		1B	39	353	34	3	26	.992					
1982	42	DH	102	0	0	0	0	N.A.					
		1B	14	116	10	0	12	1.000					
		OF	2	3	0	0	0	1.000		0	2	0	
1983	43	DH	107	0	0	0	0	N.A.					
		1B	2	22	1	0	1	1.000					
		OF	1	0	0	0	0	N.A.		1	0	0	

POSITION TOTAL

							Games Played				
Position	Games Played	Putouts	Assists	Errors	Double Plays	Fielding %		Left Field	Center Field	Right Field	Gold Glove
OF	2,076	3941	195	82	30	.981		1917	159	7	
1B	765	6459	512	41	610	.994					
DH	411	N.A.									
3B	33	37	68	12	3	.897					

PHOTO CREDITS	Page Number
ASSOCIATED PRESS	48, 56, 66
© BETTMANN/CORBIS	4, 5, 6, 11, 11, 11, 33, 57, 69, 70, 71, 73, 74, 90, 102, 105, 105, 115, 117, 124, 132, 133, 135, 141, 146, 147, 148, 149, 151, 151, 156, 157, 157, 171, 172, 173, 179, 182, 184, 185, 191, 199, 210, 220, 238
COURTESY OF THE BRIDGE HAMPTON HISTORICAL SOCIETY	12, 13, 16, 17, 19, 20
COURTESY OF DICK GORDON	Back of Endpaper Right, viii, ix, 23, 30, 39, 40, 46, 65, 74, 74, 131, 139, 196, 216, 216, 222, 222, 229, 232, 233, 235, 238, 239, Back of End Paper Left
JEAN SMITH	24, 26, 27
JIM BOURG/REUTERS/CORBIS	ii, iii
© CORBIS	69, 156
© TODD GIPSTEIN/CORBIS	204, 205
DAVID SEELIG/ICON SMI/CORBIS	iv, v, 42, 43
ART SHAY/SPORTS ILLUSTRATED	107
DICK RAPHAEL/SPORTS ILLUSTRATED	200, 206
FRED KAPLAN/SPORTS ILLUSTRATED	161
HEINZ KLUETMEIER/SPORTS ILLUSTRATED	112, 186, 197
HERB SCHARMAN/SPORTS ILLUSTRATED	75, 96, 128
JAMES DRAKE/SPORTS ILLUSTRATED	82, 196
JOHN IACONO/SPORTS ILLUSTRATED	197
LEE BALTERMAN/SPORTS ILLUSTRATED	62, 78
NEAL LEIFER/SPORTS ILLUSTRATED	125
RICHARD MACKSON/SPORTS ILLUSTRATED	202
TONY TRIOLO/SPORTS ILLUSTRATED	154, 165
WALTER IOOSS, JR/SPORTS ILLUSTRATED	10, 86, 96, 108, 136, 144, 164
FOCUS ON SPORT/GETTY IMAGES	76, 100, 101, 120, 162, 168, 174, 176, 177, 212, 224, 225
GETTY IMAGES	52, 53, 80, 192, 222
MLB PHOTOS VIA GETTY IMAGES	Front End Paper Left, Front End Paper Right, 97, 142, 236, 244, 245, Back End Paper Left and Right
TIME & LIFE PICTURES/GETTY IMAGES	89, 2, 166, x, 88
COURTESY STEW THORNLEY	58
RICHARD JOPSON	231
RICHARD LEE	i

SPECIAL THANKS TO DOUGLAS GORNEY FOR AN OUTSTANDING WRITING JOB.

BOSTON
1967 AMERICAN LE

BACK ROW: Gary Waslewski, Jose Santiago, Gary
Darrell Brandon, Russ Gibson, Sparky Lyl

MIDDLE ROW: Billy Rohr, Joe Foy, Mike Andrews
Thomas, Dalton Jones, Norm Siebern, Je
Equipment Manager Vince Orlando

FRONT ROW: Batboy Keith Rosenfield, Tony Con
Maglie, Coach Bobby Doerr, Manager Dick
Reggie Smith, George Scott, Traveling Sec
Manager Don Fitzpatrick